YOU'VE PROBABLY NOTICED THAT THERE
ARE CERTAIN TIMES OF THE YEAR WHEN
THINGS SEEM TO GO A LITTLE CRAZY

- A check you wrote bounces
- A computer virus ruins some of your files
- A friend you had planned to meet forgets the date
- The timer on your VCR doesn't work and you tape the wrong show
- You try to return a purchase but can't find the receipt
- Your cell phone just doesn't seem to work when you really need it.

THESE STRANGE HAPPENINGS MAY BE DUE TO
A PARTICULAR ALIGNMENT OF THE STARS
AND THAT SPEEDY LITTLE PLANET
CLOSEST TO THE SUN.

NOW LEARN HOW TO IDENTIFY, AVOID, AND
COMBAT . . .

MERCURY RETROGRADE

mercury retrograde

YOUR SURVIVAL GUIDE
TO ASTROLOGY'S
MOST PRECARIOUS
TIME OF YEAR!

chrissie blaze

WARNER BOOKS

An AOL Time Warner Company

Copyright © 2002 by Chrissie Blaze
All rights reserved.

Warner Books, Inc., 1271 Avenue of the Americas, New York, NY 10020
Visit our Web site at www.twbookmark.com.

 An AOL Time Warner Company

Printed in the United States of America
First Printing: April 2002
10 9 8 7 6 5 4 3 2 1

Library of Congress Cataloging-in-Publication Data

Blaze, Chrissie.
    Mercury retrograde : your survival guide to astrology's most precarious time of
year! / Chrissie Blaze.
        p. cm.
    Includes bibliographical references.
    ISBN 0-446-67765-5
    1. Astrology. I. Title.

BF1711 .B57 2001
133.5'33—dc21   2001046671

Cover design by Brigid Pearson
Book design and text composition by L & G McRee

This book is dedicated in thankfulness to my beloved Master,
Dr. George King, who always reached for the stars.

ACKNOWLEDGMENTS

I would like to thank my husband, Gary, for his love, wisdom, and support; and my parents, Phyllis and Tom Shafe, for their loving patience and for always being there for me whatever I do! I am also grateful to my relatives Esme and Valerie Williams, who first introduced me to astrology at the age of fourteen, and who have continued a lifelong love affair with this wonderful, fascinating study, as I have.

Thanks also go to my friend and agent, Sandy Choron, for her talent, inspiration, and excitement for this project; to Ron Schaumberg for his sensitive advice and practical help; and to Dave Davies for our "astro-chats." I also am grateful to John Aherne at Warner Books for believing in me, and for being so incredibly perceptive and intelligent. And my thanks go to my good friend Dr. Richard Lawrence for writing the wonderful foreword.

Finally, I would like to thank all the astrologers and people in the New Age movement—especially my friends and colleagues in The Aetherius Society—who are working hard to promote spiritual awareness and to bring light into our world.

CONTENTS

FOREWORD

I was fascinated by this eagerly awaited book on an aspect of astrology that is too often overlooked. We are all affected by Mercury Retrograde; Chrissie has now given us an effective and practical way of handling it with maximum benefit to ourselves and others.

I am glad to say I have known Chrissie as a close friend for over twenty-five years. She is one of those rare people who really live their beliefs. She does not write just from her extensive research of astrology—though her knowledge is impressive to say the least—but, more important, from her direct experience of witnessing it at work in the lives of the many people she has helped and guided over the years. Chrissie's observations on the complex patterns that interweave the cosmic matrix of our lives, are based on fact as well as theory.

Gone are the days, thank goodness, when astrology was the preserve of a few Eastern scholars and pundits who set out to determine your life for you. Now it is mainstream. You can study it at universities, it is used in business, and hardly any magazines are sold without including your horoscope—not popular ones anyway. A recent investigation at Goldsmiths College, which is part of London University, revealed that about 75 percent of people now read their horoscopes.

But this trend has its downside as well: The subject can be so trivialized as to become first superficial, then superstitious, and eventually superfluous. With an author like Chrissie Blaze this will never happen. Her style is simple in the highest sense: always understandable, but never banal. And if that isn't the secret of good writing, it's certainly one of them. But she never substitutes style for content—this is a book packed full of usable tips and pointers to a more successful and fulfilled life.

The beauty of tackling the Mercury Retrograde factor is that you can now use these times to change your life for the better. An aspect of the mysterious law called karma is that you can change what was once believed to be fated, or inevitable. Like astrology, karma is more fashionable than ever. It is amazing that an ancient Sanskrit word like this should appear in the title of rock-and-roll and rap songs in the twenty-first century. And yet not surprising really, because people instinctively know that there are forces of destiny at work in their lives that go beyond chance and the chemical makeup of their bodies.

Once people know that there are guiding forces at work, they are often far better able to cope with whatever life brings. Showing people that there is a purpose behind the apparently haphazard events of their existence is generally far more helpful to them than bucket loads of tea and sympathy. In time the sympathy evaporates with the tea—whereas the forces of destiny last forever.

Chrissie has done us all a service in focusing our attention on Mercury, which is the Roman name for the Egyptian god Thoth, known to the Greeks as Hermes. This mysterious figure, who was known from the Middle Ages onward as Hermes Trismegistus, was the pivotal figure in Western magic as practiced by such advanced luminaries as Count Saint Germain and Sir Francis Bacon. Alchemy became the watchword for these practical mystics: transmuting the metal of everyday existence into the gold of spiritual attainment.

One of the most precious of their alchemical tools was, and still is, the revelations brought to us through astrology. This book, though modern and accessible, falls into this tradition. Chrissie takes the potentially capricious elements of Mercury Retrograde and transmutes them into a force for good, in a way that is relevant to you and me and what is going on in the alchemy of our lives.

RICHARD LAWRENCE
International best-selling author of the
Little Book of Karma and others;
Britain's leading expert in the paranormal and
spiritual sciences

PREFACE

There is a growing trend, now prevalent in the United States and many other countries, to blame everything difficult, frustrating, irritating, and annoying on Mercury Retrograde. Just recently people have been asking me if Mercury is retrograde when it is not. I must admit it often feels that way, and I often find myself trying to figure out why the world has gone mad. Sometimes I have the feeling that Mercury went retrograde years ago and just forgot to go direct again! Still, despite the increasing stress of all those mercurial things, such as communication blips, I am absolutely convinced of the benefits of Mercury Retrograde—and hope to also convince you of them.

"A little bit of knowledge is a dangerous thing," I hear my friends saying. This is true, but the popular books on Sun signs have enabled many to understand themselves at a deeper level. *Mercury Retrograde* can do the same. While it is important to visit experienced, professional astrologers to receive an insightful birth chart interpretation, it is also important that we gain more control of our lives.

Astrology is a wonderful subject—ancient, mysterious, and powerful. It is not a religion that answers the "why" of existence, but it does tell us the "how." Because of this, it is important to share. Through this planetary language we can understand what the universe is saying and how we should reply. It's not the only language but it's one, along with science, religion, yoga, music, and more. All these languages help us interpret the meaning of life.

Some astrologers scorn the global addiction to computer-generated Sun-sign horoscopes, but many people find them helpful. My philosophy is: "If it works, it can't be all bad." My office colleague, a Libran, found tremendous solace post-divorce in her daily horoscope. It gave her hope and had an uncanny knack of "hitting the nail on the head" of her daily experiences. Although extremely general, there is no doubt that when the Sun enters Aries, we feel a bit perkier, and when it is in Capricorn, in January, we have more strength for our sober New Year's resolutions.

It's time to stop groaning about popularizing, for this is the age when the ancient mysteries must be demystified and put to work for the benefit of the whole. Practicality is the key; ivory towers have no place in our modern world. All of the languages of the cosmos, whether science or astrology, should have a vital, practical base from which to serve the growth and enlightenment of humankind.

One criticism of astrology is that it is not scientific. But although like every other science it is changing and evolving, the fundamental principles upon which it rests are reliable. Some critics call it "merely anecdotal" in that it rests many claims on observations of human nature. I suppose we could equally say, then, that medical science is anecdotal in that it rests many of its claims on observations of rats!

In an attempt to push astrology toward gaining credence with the scientific community, some astrologers have tended toward increased technicality. This is another path as slippery as the overpopularizing approach, for the danger here is of losing sight of the whole in a mass of increasingly complex details. So on the one hand there is the increasing popularity of astrology, and on the other its increasing complexity. In this book I aim to show that the popular approach need not debase but can be helpful and enlightening.

There is already too much emphasis on intellect in our so-called civilized world. Our educational system encourages it, and our economy rewards it. Now the pendulum must swing toward a greater emphasis on the value of intuition, compassion, understanding, enlightenment, and spiritual growth. Astrology can help provide all these things.

Hopefully, you are convinced that this ancient science has some validity today. Still, one thing I must point out (before someone else does) is that the whole basis of astrology rests on illusion. The Zodiac is based on the imaginary path of the Sun through the heavens. The Sun does not actually travel through the different signs of the Zodiac; it just appears to do so, as it passes between the Earth on which we live and the constellations. When Mercury is retrograde, this planet does not actually go backward in the heavens, but only appears to do so. More about this later . . . Just as astrology rests on illusion, however, so too do many other bodies of knowledge that we accept. In Albert Einstein's words: "Reality is merely an illusion, albeit a persistent one."

You don't need to be an astrologer to see that a major global shift is going on. All the "hard" sciences have already gone "soft." The hardest one of all was physics, but with the development of quantum theory it fell hard and is still falling. Perhaps the people we thought were scientists weren't really scientists after all! One thing a good astrologer has in common with a good quantum physicist is they both know that the universe is magical. Perhaps we are at last reaching a truly scientific view of the universe, one in which awe, wonder, and inspiration go hand in hand with observation and statistics.

As a child, you knew life was magical before you were conditioned to believe it was not. As a three-year-old, I frequently dived into the swimming pool and breathed underwater—and yet later I learned that this was impossible. Paradoxically, although the whole basis of astrology rests on illusion, it is also one of the purest studies of truth. Since it deals with the energies and forces of the cosmos, why should we expect to understand it by intellect alone? Astrology is a study of something so much greater than we are that it takes all of us—our intellect, our intuition, our inspiration—to begin to grasp it. So although astrology is as much a science as any, using it is definitely an intuitive art, through which we can learn to interpret things essentially beyond our comprehension.

Although many people find it hard to take astrology seriously, they can easily take seriously its counterpart—astronomy. *Astronomy* means "naming the stars," and *astrology* is "the logic of the stars." I know comparisons are odious, but which study sounds the greater? Astronomy represents the glove, while astrology is the living spirit of the hand inside the glove. It is strange that our analytical left-brain schools and universities teach us to make sense of the glove—while neglecting the thing that moves the hand inside it. I feel sure it will not be too long, however, before these twin sciences can once again join hands, so to speak.

Perhaps it will be soon, as astrology gains more universal acceptance through a combination of accessibility, education, and public relations. After all, most people who do not believe in it just do not have a clue what it is about. This is not really disbelief, but ignorance. Understandable, I suppose, when scientists have disregarded it and religionists have called it blasphemy.

One of the great things about astrology is that it works, despite the controversy. We may never completely understand it, but we can marvel at it—just as we marvel before the majesty of a setting sun or the relentless ebb and flow of the tides of the oceans, even though we do not really understand them.

Recently two dear people I know passed away. One was a friend, the other my uncle. Both were kind, gentle souls who had lived long, full lives. It was not really until their funerals, however, that those of us who had known them became aware of the impact they had made on our lives. They were not millionaires; they had not achieved tremendous success or fame, but they had been kind and helpful to everyone they met. Their lifelong simple acts of kindness had built two beautiful lives, and the crowds at their funerals spoke volumes. It was testimony to the fact that kindness to others is far more important than material success.

We all know these things, but can easily forget them. There is a flow to life, however, and the planets act as agents in this great cosmic flow geared to growth and evolution. If we ignore the urge to become better people, we will find the planetary influences beating us over the head to change. If we stop and listen, we can appreciate the important things in life and gain deeper understanding. Mercury Retrograde can help us do this.

Because astrology works so well, it will play an ever more important role in our future. In a desperate search for understanding, people flock to counselors, but good astrologers can reach the heart of a problem more quickly. From the client's birth chart, they can see her strengths, weaknesses, struggles, potential, and destiny. Indeed, they can see every area of her life, from what kind of relationship or career she would flourish in to what is causing her pain. Good astrologers can offer the client immediate solutions to her problems. Everything is laid out before their discerning eyes, even before they meet a client!

Learning astrology is a great idea if you are serious about your journey through life. I started my own journey of understanding at a fairly young age. I was only fourteen when my aunt, an avid astrologer and metaphysician, showed me a birth chart for the first time. The strangest thing was that when I looked at it, with no previous knowledge of astrology in this lifetime, I understood it. In that instant I received a strong impression of the person whom this chart represented. This experience left an indelible mark on me. Several years later I began to study astrology seriously, together with metaphysics and the spiritual sciences. In my twenties I enrolled in and qualified as an astrologer at the Faculty of Astrological Studies in London.

I believe that I have past-life experience of astrology, and that this was what accounted for my immediate recognition of the meanings of the astrological chart. There is also the fact that symbols are far more ancient than is language. Many people believe that prior to language, humans communicated with each other and with the animal kingdom through thought. Animals still communicate via thought and so in some ways are not as limited as we are. Thought is transmitted via symbols. It makes sense, therefore, that many ancient symbols, including the astrological ones, are impressed in the collective subconscious.

Astrology is a wonderful study that can help prepare you for life. Learning astrology is rather like learning Italian before you take a vacation in Tuscany—it will help you appreciate your trip and make the most of it. By the same token, learning about Mercury Retrograde can be equated to learning how to order lunch in Italian while in the Tuscan countryside. Without some smattering of the language, you may have a hungry, frustrating day. With it, you can enjoy lunch, your charming hosts, the beauty of Tuscany—and feel good about the whole world!

CHAPTER 7

Mercury Retrograde: A Look Back

We've all felt them . . .

Those moments when our lives seem to be going . . . backward.

It's happening everywhere, to just about everyone. For three weeks at a stretch, maybe five, communication breaks down in a thousand weird ways. Wires get crossed, messages lost. The cell phone dies in the middle of a call. A package never arrives. We sign contracts for deals that go horribly wrong. We squabble with friends or loved ones.

Most such moments are trivial in themselves—but collectively they pack a punch. The phone call we miss might have been a dream job offer. The package that never comes might contain our kid's asthma medicine. A thoughtless word can fracture a friendship.

During these times, we may feel that we just can't get on the right wavelength. We're out of sorts because we're out of synch. Trouble seems to multiply. Travel plans go terribly awry. Couples split. Accident and sickness rates soar.

Projects launched on waves of enthusiasm drown in dismal failure.

You may feel this is happening only to you. But in fact it's happening to everyone, and at the same time. Lately people all over the world are discovering that these communication slumps strike with scary regularity. Three or at most four times a year, for a stretch of twenty-two days or so, life seems to be moving in the wrong direction—busy signals, misunderstandings, missed connections. We want to crawl into bed and pull the covers over our heads.

There's good news in all of this. If you know ahead of time that these periods will occur, you can avoid disaster. Even better, you can actually *benefit* during these times. This book will show you how.

The force driving this phenomenon is no secret. In fact, we've known about it for thousands of years. You'll be reassured to learn that it's completely natural and very predictable. And oddly enough, it's both very real—and very much an illusion.

Let me explain.

These periods of disrupted communication I've been describing tend to occur when Mercury, the speedy little planet closest to the Sun, behaves in a certain way. Normally Mercury—like all the planets—moves forward in orbit. This forward movement is called *direct motion*.

But there are periods during the year when Mercury performs a fascinating little dance step. To an observer on Earth, Mercury appears to stop dead in its orbital track. Then it backs up for a while . . . stops again . . . and slowly begins to move forward once more. The time when it stops and backs up is known as *Mercury Retrograde*.

The word *retrograde* means "moving back." All the planets in the solar system go through retrograde periods. But this cosmic cha-cha is actually only an illusion. The planets never really stop rolling forward in their orbit. Through our Earth-bound telescopes, however, they appear to do so. That's because Earth is moving in its own orbit, too. I'll say more about this in the next chapter.

As an astrologer, I trace patterns in the movements of the heavens, then look for the wisdom these patterns reveal. In this realm Mercury is the planet that rules the ways we humans communicate. Mercury Retrograde—the period of about three weeks when the planet appears to reverse its course through the heavens—is a time when communication may break down.

Mercury Retrograde, or MR, can have a powerful impact on our lives. Not long ago people asked, "What's your sign?" Now it's, "How are you handling the retrograde?" People are swapping MR survival stories in e-mail, in Internet chat rooms, over lattés at Starbucks.

During the last MR my car radio quit working, so I didn't hear the news or traffic reports. A fog had caused a huge pileup on the interstate. I ended up plowing into the car in front of me. My car was totaled. I had to walk 2 miles in the dark. When I got home, I realized I'd left my house keys in the car. I just collapsed and cried . . .

I had been buddies with this guy for years. We never dated, but we could talk for hours and we laughed a lot. Then one night—it was the night that Mercury

went retrograde—I had dinner at his place and we
had a little too much wine and I ended up staying the
night. The next day we had a huge fight and now we
can't stand each other . . .

We'd been house shopping for months when finally
we found the perfect place. We negotiated like mad
for weeks and finally nailed down the deal. The day
we signed the contracts—during MR naturally—we
went to look at our property and discovered that the
pipes had burst. There was water damage on all three
floors. Our dream house had become a night-
mare . . .

I know lawyers who refuse to schedule court appearances during these periods. One Hollywood screenwriter
won't bother turning on her laptop during retrograde,
because, she says, she'll either "suffer terminal writer's
block or churn out total garbage." An officer at a U.S. naval
base refuses to stage war games during MR because he
knows that a single garbled signal could kill or maim his
troops.

Why are people suddenly realizing the impact of Mercury Retrograde? It's simple, really, when you think about
it. Never before in the history of humanity has there been
so much communication. Computers, the Web, e-mail, cell
phones, FedEx, faxes, beepers, chat rooms, satellites, 24/7
news . . . the world is a humming hive of contact. Today
we can reach out and touch virtually anyone in the world,
instantly.

The more we rely on our instant communication networks, the more vulnerable we become to the inevitable disruptions. And during MR there are disruptions aplenty. Throughout this book you'll find dozens of stories about the impact of the MR effect on our work, play, family, friends, relationships, money—every aspect of our mental, physical, and spiritual health.

Two quick stories from the pages of history make the point: The *Titanic* sank on April 15, 1912—during the peak of MR. The disaster may be the ultimate story of miscommunication. Officers on board ignored not one, not three, but *six* warnings that icebergs were in the vicinity. Another liner, the *Californian,* was less than 20 miles away, but its radio operator had gone off duty and so never received *Titanic's* SOS signals. Talk about communication breakdown!

More recently MR may have affected the course of history. A retrograde period ended on November 7, 2000— the day of the presidential election between Bush and Gore. Mercury shifted out of retrograde at about 9 P.M.— just *after* the TV news stations wrongly predicted that Gore would win in Florida. For more than a month afterward the breakdown in voting systems bred chaos and court battles. The election fiasco serves as a warning: Mercury is retrograde only for a little while—but MR effects can reverberate forever.

But does MR mean that we poor Earthlings, like *Titanic's* hapless passengers, are doomed? That for three weeks, three times a year, we have no choice but to suffer communication meltdown?

Not at all. By knowing what MR means and when it will occur, you can protect yourself—and others—from many of its effects. This book will show you how. In appendix 1 you'll find an *ephemeris.* It's a schedule of retrograde periods past and future. Check to see when the next will occur—it's no more than four months from now.

But seen from the right aspect, MR̥ is not a catastrophe but a gift. Mercury's pattern shows us that, in nature, there's wisdom in slowing down every so often, taking a few steps back, and reconsidering how—and when—to move forward again. In the realm of communication, retrograde serves as a reminder to "back up our data"—to double-check to see that our messages are getting through. By discovering and embracing this planetary teaching, you can make your life happier, healthier, more fulfilling in any ways you can imagine.

A lot of people misunderstand the power of astrology. They think that the planets rule our lives; that we are helpless victims of forces beyond our control. Sadly, some people use astrology as an excuse for their failures or shortcomings. "I can't help it if I screwed up! Mercury Retrograde made me do it!"

The truth is, astrology doesn't control our lives. Instead it offers a guide to the different types of energies present in the universe—the cosmic currents that shape our lives. The planets reflect aspects of our human nature. The stars don't "make" us do anything. We are ultimately responsible for choosing how to plug into, and respond to, these universal energies.

If you understand the MR̥ effect, you can shield yourself from communication snafus. The secret is simple: Just take a step back. The *re-* in *retrograde* reminds us that MR̥ is a good time to review, revisit, rethink—reboot!

Complete the following survey. Your answers will show you how M℞ affects your life.

THINKING BACK:
The M℞ Effect Survey

How does Mercury Retrograde affect you? Read through the list. If you experienced any of these events during the last Mercury Retrograde period, place up to three marks next to the item:

- Score one ℞ if you noticed the event.
- Score another ℞ if the event occurred twice or more.
- Score a third ℞ if the event caused another problem.

Here are some examples.

- A few weeks back Carol missed her flight. The delay caused her to miss her connection. As a result of the delays, she had to cancel her big job interview. Total score: 3 ℞.

- John wanted to videotape the first two games of the 2000 World Series. Both times he set the VCR wrong and ended up taping C-SPAN instead. He was annoyed, but it wasn't that big a deal. His score: 2 ℞.

Add the number of marks. If you scored:

- Less than 25 points: Either M℞ doesn't affect you much, or you're already taking steps to avoid falling into the M℞ trap!

- 25–50 points: You have normal **M℞** problems.

- 50–75 points: You might want to consider taking steps to minimize the disruption of communication breakdowns during **M℞** periods.

- 75–100 points: Look on the bright side: You're sensitive! You are particularly vulnerable to the disruptive effects of **M℞**. Take special note of the suggestions in this book for taking back your life during these periods, and make **M℞** a really positive experience.

M℞ Effects

_____ A cell phone call got cut off.

_____ I bought new batteries but they didn't work.

_____ Faxes came through garbled or smeared.

_____ People complained that I didn't listen to them.

_____ Mail I expected arrived late or not at all.

_____ I lost cable TV service for more than five minutes.

_____ I was unable to connect to the Internet when I needed to.

_____ My Internet connection was much slower than usual.

_____ I agreed to meet a friend but we each ended up at different locations.

_____ My mate and I had a fight.

_____ A check I wrote bounced.

_____ A check I deposited took a month to clear.

_____ A computer virus ruined some of my files.

_____ I backed up my computer files but something went wrong in the process.

_____ I had a car accident.

_____ My pet misbehaved.

_____ The weather report I usually rely on was totally wrong.

_____ I struggled to finish a project.

_____ I became really tongue-tied talking to my boss or coworkers.

_____ I had big arguments over misunderstood words.

_____ I broke up with my partner.

_____ A package arrived late.

_____ A package contained things I didn't order.

_____ A package never came.

_____ My glasses or contacts bothered me more than usual.

_____ The copy machine ran out of toner in the middle of a job.

_____ I had an embarrassing argument with a store clerk.

_____ I asked someone for directions and got wrong information.

_____ My boss turned down my request for promotion or a raise.

_____ My commute took at least 20 percent more time.

_____ My car had electrical problems.

_____ A close relative reported bad news in the family.

_____ A friend or family member became seriously ill.

_____ I or people I know suffered cuts, bruises, or broken bones.

_____ There were some problems with my medical records.

_____ I filled out forms but they had missing or wrong information.

_____ Copies of magazines or newspapers I subscribed to didn't arrive.

_____ I set the timer on my VCR but taped the wrong show.

_____ My clocks displayed the wrong time.

_____ I paid bills but the payments arrived late.

_____ There were errors on my bank statements.

_____ An appointment got canceled.

_____ I got a traffic ticket.

_____ I dialed a wrong number and had to speak with someone I was trying to avoid.

_____ Keys on my computer keyboard got stuck.

_____ Letters I mailed got returned for missing postage or wrong addresses.

_____ I made an expensive mistake in simple math.

_____ I made a recipe but got some of the ingredients or amounts wrong.

_____ The ATM machine swallowed my bank card.

_____ I misread a bus, train, or airline schedule.

_____ A flight I was booked on got canceled or delayed.

_____ My bag got lost during a flight.

_____ A new CD or computer disk wouldn't run on my machine.

_____ I got booted off my Internet connection for no reason.

_____ I lost my keys or my wallet.

_____ I waited on hold for a long time and then got disconnected.

_____ I bought clothes that fit fine in the store but didn't fit at home.

_____ My cell phone rang at an embarrassing moment.

_____ I set my alarm but it went off at the wrong time.

_____ Someone saw an e-mail I wanted to keep secret.

_____ I opened a fortune cookie but there was no fortune.

_____ I picked up my dry cleaning but items were missing.

_____ Food I bought was spoiled before the expiration date.

_____ I forgot someone's name as soon as I was introduced.

_____ The dial tone on my phone went out.

_____ I went to a movie but the newspaper had printed the wrong show times.

_____ The restaurant was out of everything I wanted to order.

_____ I tossed coins into the toll basket but they missed.

_____ Tape from a cassette got snarled in the player.

_____ An event I bought tickets for got canceled.

_____ My mail was delivered to a neighbor's house.

_____ I tried to return something I bought but couldn't find the receipts I'd saved.

_____ My bank balance dropped too low and I was hit with service charges.

_____ A program I'd been planning to watch was pre-empted by news events.

_____ I repeatedly pressed wrong choices when replying to a telephone voice menu.

_____ I had to take someone I care for to the emergency room.

_____ I took a wrong dose or type of medication.

_____ I forgot to buy an essential item from my grocery list.

_____ I brought too many items to the express checkout line.

_____ I had to pay library fines for late or lost books.

_____ My pen ran out of ink.

_____ I missed an event by a few minutes.

_____ A warranty expired just when I needed service.

_____ The insurance company didn't receive my premium payment.

_____ My paycheck had the wrong deductions.

_____ I received important mail addressed to someone else.

_____ My car wouldn't start.

_____ I got stood up for a date.

_____ A restaurant tab contained serious errors.

_____ A friend took a joke wrong.

_____ The pharmacist gave me the wrong prescription.

_____ I made a purchase, then realized I didn't have cash or a credit card on me.

_____ I received printed materials (checkbooks, stationery) with my name spelled wrong.

_____ One or both of the speakers in my stereo quit working.

_____ My neighborhood experienced a power outage.

_____ My hotel reservations got screwed up.

_____ I got off at the wrong exit.

_____ A store refused to accept its coupon.

_____ I lost an important phone number.

_____ Someone spread a false rumor about me.

My Score: _____

CHAPTER 2

MR: What in Heaven's Name Is Going On?

From the Mercury Retrograde casebook:

Estelle is a Los Angeles–based writer for a well-known magazine. Not long ago she was asked to cover a story in Chicago. Her flight home was scheduled to leave—*during the peak of MR*. "If I had known that," Estelle told me later, "I would never have accepted this assignment."

When she arrived at the airport, she discovered her flight had been canceled. The airline managed to book her onto a later flight—but before it took off, the pilot reported trouble with the engine and the plane returned to the terminal. The next scheduled flight wasn't until early the next morning, so the airline agreed to put Estelle up at a hotel for the night.

Through a computer snafu, the hotel was overbooked, and Estelle wound up sleeping on a roll-away bed in a room shared by two other people—complete strangers, all of them, none of whom spoke a language in common. The next morning her alarm failed to go off, and the hotel neglected to give her the wake-up call she'd requested. She ordered breakfast from room service—but her meal was delivered to the wrong room.

She finally got a seat on a flight back to L.A. The car service had arrived to pick her up at the airport, but the driver was holding a sign with her name so badly misspelled that she didn't realize she was waiting for her. To cap it all off, one of her suitcases is *still* lost. "As far as I know," said Estelle, "it's in orbit around Mercury."

Here's another tale of M℞ woe:

Peter reported to his doctor for his annual physical. He felt fine, had no complaints. But a few days later—you won't be surprised to learn it was during M℞—his doctor called him with some troubling news. One of his arteries was badly blocked. If Peter didn't have surgery almost immediately, he was likely to have a massive—potentially fatal—heart attack. Frightened, Peter hastily checked into the hospital. He was within a few minutes of being wheeled into the operating room when his doctor came to his bedside. "I have good news and bad news," she said, somewhat sheepishly. "The bad news is, there's been a mistake—my nurse mixed up your records with someone else's. The good news is, you don't need surgery. Get dressed and get out—you're fit as a fiddle." "On the drive home," Peter said, "I made two vows: One, switch doctors. Two, never schedule a checkup during M℞!"

Another story, this one with a happy ending:

Sondra, a stock trader, was excited about a new high-tech company that had developed an advanced system for building computer networks. But her heart sank when she saw the company had scheduled its initial public stock offering on the day Mercury was to go retrograde. She advised her clients not to invest, at least for a month. Sure enough, on the day the company opened its trading, its stock closed far below its original asking price. Four weeks later the stock had hit rock bottom, trading for mere pennies a share. Just as Mercury went direct again, Sondra called her clients and urged them to buy. In the days that followed, the stock soared. The investors all made small fortunes—and, because of her commissions, so did Sondra.

How can this be? Why are there times during the year when communication seems to go so wrong? And why can such a tiny, faraway planet be involved in such huge disruptions in our daily lives?

To answer, I'll take you on a quick trip through time and space. By looking at astrology's past we can understand better why its influence is so strong today. This book, of course, is about what happens when Mercury goes retrograde. It's not meant to be a complete guide to astrology, but knowing some of the basic ideas underlying this ancient art will help you make sense of Mercury's influence. You'll learn more about this in the next chapter.

A BRIEF HISTORY OF ASTROLOGY

Stargazing is among humanity's oldest arts. Though they didn't have telescopes, people of ancient civilizations could see the motions of the heavens. And they certainly felt their effects—the winds, the tides, night, day, the seasons.

One of these cosmic forces is Mercury. To the ancient

Greeks and Romans, Mercury was the god who governs a vital human urge: the urge to communicate. The planet named for this god behaves strangely at times by running backward in its orbit. When it does, communication chaos reigns. In a world as wired as our own, the potential for calamity is enormous.

The astrology familiar today in the West began in Mesopotamia, the "cradle of civilization," around 2000 B.C.E. From its earliest days, astrology combined religion and science. Astrologers were priests, trained to read the heavens as signs of divine intent. Over the centuries kings, pharaohs, and emperors relied on astrologers to tell them when the time was right to start a war, plant crops, or marry the princess next door.

Astrological readings depend on our ability to calculate and predict celestial traffic patterns. The ancients may have lacked our modern tools, but they still managed to figure out ingenious ways to practice their craft. Stonehenge, built thousands of years ago in southern England, appears to be both a temple for worship and a giant "calculator" designed to determine the position of the Sun, the Moon, and the stars. Using this tool, the ancients could predict the moment of the vernal equinox—the exact beginning of the astrological year.

Even in those days seers knew there were periods when the planets seemed to run backward in their course. They usually interpreted these retrograde events as times when disaster was likely to occur.

Over the millennia, many of civilization's leading scientific minds have incorporated astrology into their wisdom in one way or another. Hermes Trismegistus, an Egyptian priest-astrologer (circa 2000 B.C.E.), is famous for a pronouncement that not only was carved in stone (hieroglyphics, no less) but has also become the basis for astrology and many major religious philosophies: "What is below is like that which is above, and that which is above is like that which is below."

In the Greek world Pythagoras (born about 600 B.C.E.) was an expert mathematician who believed that "the world is built upon the power of numbers." Like Hermes of Egypt, Pythagoras taught his followers about the interrelationship of all things in the universe. Hippocrates, known as the father of medicine, believed that his patients' emotional, mental, and physical well-being was determined by the positions of the planets at birth. The philosopher Aristotle, echoing Hermes the Egyptian, wrote: "This world is inescapably linked to the motion of the world above. All power in this world is ruled by these heavenly motions."

Our modern notion of the Zodiac began with Ptolemy, the greatest scientific mind of ancient times. He was born in Egypt around the year 85 C.E. He wrote a thirteen-volume encyclopedia of mathematical teachings that showed how to calculate the movements of the planets. He then summarized these teachings in a book (well, scroll really) of astrology aimed at general readers. In this work he described the effects that the heavenly bodies have on people's lives. It's worth noting that Ptolemy described Mercury as "the ruler of the rational soul that brings riches through elegance and grace."

For hundreds of years the intellectual capital of the ancient world was Alexandria, Egypt, the city founded by Alexander the Great in the third century B.C.E. In Alexandria's great library were to be found thousands of scrolls, the accumulated wisdom of the ages. Many of these texts dealt with astrological matters. But in the fourth century C.E. Christianity became the official religion of the Roman Empire. Christian clerics had little tolerance for astrology, which they equated with witchcraft. In 415 C.E. a band of monks rioted to protest pagan influence. During their spree, they came across a woman named Hypatia, daughter of the library's last great mathematician and herself a noted mathematician and astronomer. Because she was a pagan, the angry monks dragged her to the library and burned her as a witch. The fire destroyed most of the library's holdings. Two and a half centuries later, when Alexandria had fallen under the control of Islamic priests, the last of the library's priceless documents were burned as fuel to heat water in the bathhouses. Much ancient wisdom, including the teachings of astrology, disappeared literally in a puff of smoke, and the shadow of the Dark Ages fell across the Western world.

Things brightened up during the Renaissance, the rebirth of learning and art modeled on the rediscovered teachings of ancient Greece and Rome. In the thirteenth century Roger Bacon, an English friar and scientist, believed that astrology could be used to foretell the future and that it was a valuable instrument for personal and global transmutation. Geniuses such as Paracelsus, a German-Swiss chemist who discovered that disease was caused by outside forces, and Leonardo da Vinci, artist and philosopher, all used elements of astrology in their work.

The greatest astrologer of the age was Nostradamus, born in France in 1507. A devout and charitable man of the church, he was famous for his uncanny predictions. He attributed his prophetic skill to a combination of inspiration and advanced astrological calculation.

Other leading scientists also explored astrological concepts. Copernicus, who proved that the Sun—not Earth—was at the center of the solar system, was both an astronomer and an astrologer. Tycho Brahe, a Danish scientist, lectured on astrology at the University of Copenhagen. Brahe devised the ephemeris, a table that calculates planetary motion. (Part of Brahe's legacy, an ephemeris for Mercury Retrograde, appears at the back of this book.) Johannes Kepler is famous for devising the laws of planetary motion. He believed that the positions of heavenly bodies (astrological aspects) held sway over events on Earth, but he did not believe that predictions were possible. Isaac Newton, who identified the laws of gravity and motion, studied alchemy and astrology. According to legend, he answered a critic of astrology with the retort, "Sir, I have studied it—*you* have not."

Interest in astrology increased each time new planets were discovered: Uranus in 1781, Neptune in 1846, and Pluto in 1930.

Today millions of people around the world consult astrologers for advice and insight into the human psyche and spirit. Perhaps the most influential astrologer of our own time is Dane Rudhyar, who in 1969 developed an approach known as humanistic astrology. His method doesn't rely on devising proofs that planetary motions directly cause events. Instead, humanistic astrologers regard the dance of the planets as a rich and elegant symbolic language. Like the medicine wheel of the Native Americans or the mandala of Buddhist practice, humanistic astrology explores the many aspects of the human spirit. From this modern perspective, the stars and planets don't dictate who we are or what will happen to us. Instead, astrology becomes a multifaceted mirror that allows us to confront ourselves, explore our inner being, and decide what path we will take to best serve ourselves, our loved ones, and our planet.

Through the modern science of radio astronomy, we see more of the universe than the ancients could, and we measure its churning, explosive activity with astounding precision. Many modern discoveries confirm and expand what the ancients had already discovered to be an essential truth: that bodies in motion exert enormous influence on each other, even at great distances. On one extreme of the scale are the planets in their cosmic ballet. On the other are atoms and their particles. Somewhere in the middle of the scale is us. We humans, too, are bodies in motion—and not just bodies, but minds and souls as well.

THE ZODIAC

The Zodiac is like an imaginary belt drawn around the celestial sphere. Picture Earth as a marble suspended inside a glass bowl. Now think of the constellations as having been painted on the bowl's surface. The Zodiac, like Earth's equator, is a circle around the middle of the bowl. Like any circle, the Zodiac can be divided into 360 degrees. Each of the twelve signs of the Zodiac occupies thirty degrees and contains one major constellation.

Imagine yourself standing on Earth, facing south, at night. Ahead of you, at the farthest range of your vision, is the horizon. Turn your head to the left—to the east. Now imagine looking up, directly overhead, and then to the west. You've just scanned half of the Zodiac. Because Earth is turning, the signs of the Zodiac constantly wheel overhead. And because Earth orbits the Sun, the constellations that appear in the night sky constantly change positions as well.

BIRTH CHARTS

Astrology is a rich and complex subject. It teaches us that the alignment of the planets, the Sun, the Moon, and other celestial bodies can have powerful influence over our lives. How this influence will play out over time is related to the moment of your birth. If you consult a professional astrologer, it helps to know the exact date and time and your precise geographic location at the moment you were born. With this information, an astrologer can develop and interpret your *birth chart*—a diagram that identifies the precise positions of the astrological bodies in relation to each other's positions in the Zodiac at the moment you made your debut on Earth.

More than that, your birth chart is a diagram of you. It shows your potential and can help guide you toward your future. The birth chart is vitally important. It is as personal to you and as unique as is your fingerprint—and yet it reveals so much more. To the experienced and talented astrologer, your birth chart indicates not only your physical, emotional, and mental tendencies; your habits, personality, career, resources, relationships, and more—but also your spiritual aspirations.

One thing that your birth chart cannot do, however, is show *how* you will live your life. You have to make this choice, and you decide every day whether you will use your vast potential, your inner resources, and your love—or waste them. An understanding of your birth chart can point toward realizing a more creative, positive, balanced, and authentic you: the you that knows no fears and no limits. The you that is a living, breathing, evolving part of the universe in which we live.

A typical birth chart is drawn in the shape of a wheel divided into twelve segments. These segments represent the Houses (see below). A line drawn across the middle of the chart, called the *horizon,* divides the wheel into upper and lower halves. This represents the position of the Zodiac at the time of your birth. The top half is essentially the daytime sky. (The stars and planets are there, of course; you just can't see them.) The bottom half represents the nighttime sky, visible at the moment of your birth to people on the other side of the planet.

Some people refer to a birth chart (also called a natal chart) as the horoscope. Your birth chart reflects your history—your astrological starting point—and also indicates your future potential. Astrologers can build on this information to provide insights into current moments and possible future trends.

SUN SIGNS

The birth chart documents the major astrological forces at work in your life and how you may interpret these. You can, however, take just a single aspect from the complexity of your birth chart—such as your Sun sign—and still learn a lot about yourself. Your Sun sign is the position along the ecliptic[1] in which the Sun was positioned when you were born. Many people, even those with little interest in astrology, are familiar with the concept of the Sun sign. "I'm a Libra," they said, or "I'm a Scorpio."

Broadly speaking, the Sun signs reflect your creative potential and character. People with the same Sun sign tend to have certain major personality traits in common. But it's too simplistic to say that "all Sagittarians are alike." There are far too many forces at work in the heavens for this to be true! For one thing, we all have *each* of the Sun signs in our chart at some point and to some degree of influence. It would take another entire book to describe the Sun signs in any detail. But table 1 provides a brief (and somewhat simplified) glance.

[1] The path followed by the Sun and planets as they move across the sky. It is like a band surrounding Earth that is divided into twelve segments for each sign of the Zodiac, from Aries through Pisces.

TABLE 1:
Sun Signs and Their Meaning

Name	Symbol	Icon	Dates	General Qualities
Aries	Ram	A	March 21–April 19	Dynamic; leader of the pack; the ideas person; prefers to initiate rather than complete; pioneering; creative; impulsive; honest; to the point
Taurus	Bull	B	April 20–May 20	Grounded; persistent; dogged; resourceful; a knack for money and business; with keen senses; typically art lovers, gourmets, healers
Gemini	Twins	C	May 21–June 21	Intellectually inclined; probing; bright; quick witted; love to rationalize; imaginative; flexible; dexterous; communicative
Cancer	Crab	D	June 22–July 22	Nurturing; home loving; family oriented; patriotic; communal; retentive memory; sensitive
Leo	Lion	E	July 23–Aug. 22	Dramatic; creative; strong in purpose; able to see the whole picture; delegators; inspirational; natural leaders; dignified; opinionated; warm; generous

Virgo	Virgin	F	Aug. 23–Sept. 22	Love to serve; strong sense of duty; industrious; methodical; efficient; multitalented; detail oriented; modest; practical; reliable
Libra	Scales	G	Sept. 23–Oct. 22	Focused on others; strong partners; balanced; value harmony and fair play; sociable; objective; believers in the common good
Scorpio	Scorpion	H	Oct. 23–Nov. 21	Serious; focused; probing; secretive; intuitive; intense; resourceful; passionate; possessed of regenerative powers
Sagittarius	Hunter	I	Nov. 22–Dec. 21	Truth seeking; adventurous; broad minded; philosophical; religious; clear thinkers; lovers of freedom and movement
Capricorn	Goat	J	Dec. 22–Jan. 19	Businesslike; ambitious; determined; hardworking; industrious; efficient; patient; disciplined; methodical
Aquarius	Water bearer	K	Jan. 20–Feb. 18	Humanitarian; philanthropic; progressive; forward thinking; inventive; original; freedom loving; individualistic
Pisces	Fish	L	Feb. 19–March 20	Selfless; spiritual; feeling oriented; intuitive; compassionate; kind; charitable; self-sacrificing

PLANETS

As important as the Sun signs are, they represent only a part of the astrological story. With the exception of the Sun, the Moon is the most influential of the planets. Because of its swift orbit around Earth, it travels through the entire Zodiac in about twenty-eight days. The Moon governs your moods and habits. And in this regard it is a major influence on how you relate to other people—and how they relate to you.

The planets constitute another important set of influences. In astrology the word *planet* refers to the orbiting bodies of the solar system as well as the Sun and the Moon. The latter two are often referred to as the *luminaries,* or lights, because they are the major sources of illumination. (Strictly speaking, of course, the Sun and the Moon are not planets.)

The planets represent different types of energies that combine, compete, and conspire to make you the person you are. The position of all the planets in your birth chart is extremely important—and this planetary dynamic affects you throughout your life. Also, as the planets move through the heavens—some quickly, like the Moon and Mercury, and some extremely slowly, like Uranus and Pluto—they have different effects upon you, bringing different experiences and challenges to the fore.

I've already mentioned a little bit about Mercury and its influence over communication. A quick summary of all the planetary energies follows.

TABLE 2:
Planets and Their Energies

☉ Sun	The self, ego, individuality, willpower
☽ Moon	Emotions, feelings, habits, moods
☿ Mercury	Communication, intellect, awareness
♀ Venus	Harmony, love, relationships, artistic awareness
♂ Mars	Physical strength, energy, drive, determination
♃ Jupiter	Exploration, generosity, optimism, benevolence
♄ Saturn	Discipline, structure, responsibility, wisdom
♅ Uranus	Originality, humanitarianism, revolution, freedom
♆ Neptune	Spirituality, sensitivity, compassion
♇ Pluto	Transformation, regeneration, rebirth

Sun

The Sun is the center of our solar system—and it is our center. It is the star without whose radiant energy there would be no life. Your Sun sign represents the way you express your vital spirit, or creative drive; it provides the fuel for your inner fire. Where the Sun is in your chart is like the identity tag that describes how you express your core self.

Moon

Unlike the constancy of the Sun, the Moon represents your ever-changing response to life. Your Moon sign reveals your emotional reactions, habits, and instincts and the adjustment of your inner sense of purpose (Sun) to the necessities of life. The Moon represents your subconscious; together with the Sun, these two luminaries are like celestial partners that you use to rule your life.

Mercury

This tricky fast-moving planet symbolizes movement and communication. Where Mercury appears in your birth charts shows whether you talk sparingly, slowly, and methodically or whether you like to chat up a breeze. It's the way you think, gather facts, and process information, and your ability to use words.

Venus

Astrologers associate Venus with love, beauty, art, harmony, and pleasure. Where Venus is in your birth chart describes the quality of your relationships with others and how you express your affection—or otherwise. Venus in your birth chart governs your artistic impulses, describes what gives you pleasure, and reveals how you handle your money.

Mars

Mars in your birth chart indicates the manner in which you take the initiative and dive into new things. Do you delicately put out one toe to test the temperature of the water, or do you dive right in? While Venus represents the power of harmony and balance, Mars represents the power of assertion; your outward expression of energy. Early astrologers associated Mars with war. It is up to you, however, whether you choose to manifest the raw energy of Mars as anger and aggression, or as a force for action and creativity.

Jupiter

This, the largest planet in our solar system, is not surprisingly associated with those things that bring expansion to your life. It represents opportunity, travel, growth, abundance, as well as optimism and good cheer. Whatever

Jupiter touches, it expands; like all the other planets, it can express itself positively or negatively. It can bring generosity and good luck, or excess and laziness. Again, it is up to you how you use the wonderful energies of Jupiter.

Saturn

Unlike Jupiter, the influence of Saturn is somber and serious. It represents discipline and the structure and foundations of your life. The old astrologers gave this planet a bad reputation, but it can be your greatest teacher. Where Saturn is in your birth chart, you may feel weak and lacking, but if you regard life's lessons as opportunities for growth, Saturn will become your friend. Saturn urges you toward success through hard work, perseverance, and discipline. By using the energies of Saturn wisely, you will find true confidence replacing your fears and vulnerabilities.

Uranus

Whereas Saturn represents restrictions in your life, the planet Uranus represents the urge for freedom from restrictions—physical, mental and emotional. This slow-moving planet, known along with Neptune and Pluto as one of the transpersonal planets, is the planet of revolution. Where it is in your birth chart indicates where your individuality is expressed. It determines the area of your life in which you can expect the unexpected.

Neptune

Neptune is elusive and difficult to define. The influence of this planet in your birth chart stretches beyond the practical, everyday world into the realm of intuition, psychic ability, and the imagination. It brings compassion and dissolves boundaries that divide us. It sensitizes and spiritualizes—but if we choose to use the negative side of its inspirational energies, it brings deceit, illusion, and confusion.

Pluto

Pluto is the most distant planet in our solar system, but its effects are profound. Where Pluto is in your birth chart is where you feel the power to regenerate. Pluto gives you the desire to change world conditions and to overcome the hardest of obstacles in your own life. The positive use of this powerful energy is as a healer or psychologist, but a person who uses Pluto power negatively can be a willful, ruthless tyrant. Pluto represents power, rebirth, and trans-formation.

I want to emphasize that these planetary qualities should not be regarded as "positive" or "negative" in and of themselves. Instead, these qualities are tools that we can use in positive or negative ways, depending on our personalities, needs, goals, and desires. As an analogy drawn from the realm of Mercury, the pen with which I write is neither positive nor negative. I can use it to write a loving letter to my husband—or to write a sarcastic and angry note to a coworker. The pen itself is neutral. It's how I choose to *use* the tool that determines its quality.

HOUSES

The birth chart also contains twelve segments called Houses. One way to put the components of your astrological chart into a real-world context is to look at the twelve Houses of the Zodiac. Each of these sectors of the Zodiac deals with a different aspect of your life. By examining the placement of the planets and signs in the various Houses, the image of your astrological makeup is further sharpened.

The first sign of the Zodiac, Aries, is the ruler of the First House; Taurus, the second sign, rules the Second House; and so on around your birth chart. Any of the twelve signs can visit a particular House and add its own characteristics to it, based on time, date, and place of birth. It would be correct to infer that the Houses possess traits similar to those of the signs of the Zodiac that rule them, as well as taking on traits of each planet that travels through them. While the signs deal with inner qualities relating to the self, however, the Houses relate to various areas of life's activities and needs, such as career, home, friends, and family.

The qualities of the Houses add depth and dimension to our ability to understand ourselves in astrological terms. If, for example, your chart finds Uranus, known as the planet of rebellion, in the First House—the House of Self—you may seem a little odd to others because you wear your individuality on the surface. If you have the conservative planet Saturn placed there, others will see you as a solid citizen.

Over the course of time, the planets move into and out of the Houses in infinite permutations, usually in direct motion, sometimes in retrograde. Their various energies combine to influence the environments through which we pass during the course of our day.

What follows is a brief summary of the meanings of each of the twelve Houses or "departments" of your life. For further explanation, please refer to chapter 4.

First House (Ascendant)—House of Self

The Ascendant is one of the most important factors in your birth chart (along with the Sun and Moon). The Ascendant is the sign at the beginning of your First House, and it reveals a lot about your temperament and constitution. Who are you? How do you realize your best self? The Ascendant describes your physical presence and how you present yourself to the world.

The First House is ruled by the sign Aries and the planet Mars.

Second House—Values and Possessions

The Second House shows your material circumstances as well as your acquisitive urge, how you deal with possessions, and your relationship to your own body. It is not limited to tangible things, however, but is also connected to your feelings, resources, and value system.

The Second House is ruled by the sign Taurus and the
planet Venus.

TABLE 3: The Houses	
First House	Self
Second House	Values and resources
Third House	Communication
Fourth House	Home
Fifth House	Creativity
Sixth House	Work and health
Seventh House	Relationships
Eighth House	Security and shared resources
Ninth House	Travel
Tenth House	Career
Eleventh House	Friends and ideals
Twelfth House	Inner self

Third House—Communication

The Third House indicates the manner in which you communicate on an everyday level and the relationships that determine your daily life. It represents your siblings, neighbors, and kindred spirits as well as your early education in life.

The Third House is ruled by the sign Gemini and the planet Mercury.

Fourth House—Roots and Home

The Fourth House describes your origins, your parental home, and the circumstances influencing your childhood and youth. It describes how you relate to your family and home. It represents the type of sanctuary you create in your home for yourself and others as well as the sanctuary you create within you.

The Fourth House is ruled by the sign Cancer and the Moon.

Fifth House—Pleasure and Creativity

The Fifth House represents all types of creative expression. It indicates how you relate to children, pleasure, and simple fun. It shows how you find emotional satisfaction and is sometimes linked to gambling; it is your willingness (or not) to take risk—on love, on money, or in life.

The Fifth House is ruled by the sign Leo and the Sun.

Sixth House—Work and Health

The Sixth House describes your daily life and routines, including your work environment, and indicates your attitude toward your subordinates and the service you give to others. It is also related to your health, diet, fitness, bodily hygiene and care, and shows tendencies toward certain illnesses.

The Sixth House is ruled by the sign Virgo and the planet Mercury.

Seventh House—Partnerships and Relating

The Descendant is the sign at the beginning of your Seventh House. This shows how you select your partners and describes the type of partnerships and relationships you seek. With this House, we see a shift away from the self toward another.

The Seventh House is ruled by the sign Libra and the planet Venus.

Eighth House—Shared Resources and Transformation

The Eighth House is commonly referred to as the House of Sex and Rebirth. It also delves into our sharing with each other on financial, emotional, and spiritual levels. It describes the transformation that takes place through our relationships, as well as the constraints.

The Eighth House is ruled by the sign Scorpio and the planets Mars and Pluto.

Ninth House—Travel and Philosophy

The Ninth House shows how you explore and seek truth and describes your philosophy of life and global outlook. It indicates travel to foreign countries, mental travel through higher education, as well as your spiritual journey. It addresses publishing and multinational ventures.

The Ninth House is ruled by the sign Sagittarius and the planet Jupiter.

Tenth House—Career and Social Status

The Tenth House describes your choice of career and your sense of vocation. It influences your general development in life and what you may become. It also represents your prestige and standing in society.

The Tenth House is ruled by the sign Capricorn and the planet Saturn.

Eleventh House—Friends and Ideals

The Eleventh House describes your friends and teachers and how you relate to the people you like and from whom you learn. It indicates how you relate to society and your humanitarian ideals. It shows the types of clubs, groups, or organizations to which you are drawn and the activities you undertake in these groups.

The Eleventh House is ruled by the sign Aquarius and the planets Saturn and Uranus.

Twelfth House—Beyond the Personal

The Twelfth House is the House of reckoning, since it is in this House that we review what we have been (and done) and decide where to go from there. It is the House of spirituality that offers compassion and transformation—or limitation and confinement, depending upon your ability to deal with the tests you face.

The Twelfth House is ruled by the sign Pisces and the planets Jupiter and Neptune.

TABLE 4:
The Birth Chart with Twelve Houses

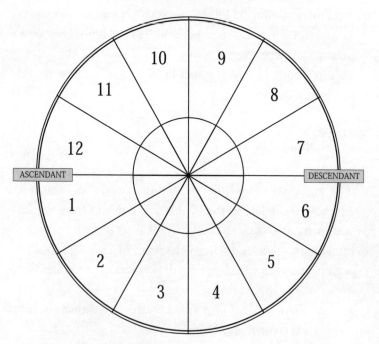

ASCENDANTS

One important key to your personality is the *Ascendant,* also known as the Rising Sign. This is the sign that was coming up on the eastern horizon at the moment you took your first breath. The Rising Sign at the beginning of the First House is positioned on the left of the chart, at the horizon in the nine o'clock position and moving south to eight o'clock. The Second House begins at the eight o'clock position, the Third House at seven o'clock, and so on around the chart wheel.

The Ascendant reflects the way you present yourself to the world and react with the environment, your self-awareness, and the way you express your personality. It also serves as a mask through which you hide parts of your inner self that you don't feel like revealing. The Ascendant is just as important in your horoscope as the Sun and the Moon. At the very least, it is important to know about these three aspects of your birth chart.

Sun-sign astrology is very limited. Knowing your Sun sign is helpful, but it categorizes you as one of only twelve different types and is therefore very general. If you know your Sun and Moon signs, you become one in 144. If you have an understanding of your Sun, Moon, and Ascendant, you become one in 1,728! Obviously, the more you under-stand about all the planets, Houses, and other aspects of your birth chart, the more you understand the unique person you really are.

For example, you may have the Sun in Pisces and dis-agree with astrology books when they tell you how shy and retiring you are. If you also have your Ascendant in Leo, however, you may be quite flamboyant, and the combination of Pisces Sun and Leo Ascendant can produce a good actor. The Sun in Pisces would give you the sensitivity to understand and slip into the roles you play, and the Leo Ascendant the confidence to express yourself dramatically in front of other people.

What follows is a quick summary of the different Ascendants from Aries to Pisces.

Aries Ascendant

You are a fiery spirit who likes to take action. You have a desire to be first as a leader of others and an idea person. You are courageous and quick off the mark. You can sometimes act without thought.

Taurus Ascendant

You are an easygoing spirit who likes to wait for things to work out. You are calm and serene, warm and friendly—but stubborn under pressure. You are artistic. You can become too attached to material possessions.

Gemini Ascendant

You are a blithe spirit who likes to communicate. You are flexible, changeable, and perceptive, but find it hard to stay with one thing for long. You can be a good teacher if you are true to your own thoughts.

Cancer Ascendant

You are a caring spirit who likes to nurture. You are extremely sensitive with a strong feeling nature. You can withdraw into your shell. A stable, loving, secure home life helps give you confidence.

Leo Ascendant

You are a dramatic spirit who likes to get attention. You are strong and confident, impressing others with your optimism and generosity. You have good leadership qualities if you learn the difference between appearance and true substance.

Virgo Ascendant

You are a practical spirit who likes to analyze. You are orderly and organized with common sense, but there is a tendency to fuss over unimportant details. You are incisive, intelligent, and discriminating, but can be overly self-critical.

Libra Ascendant

You are a cooperative spirit who likes to socialize. You have good manners, charm, and a love of harmony and beauty. You are a peacemaker—but can be too much of a people pleaser. You need to learn self-assertiveness.

Scorpio Ascendant

You are an intense spirit who likes to be thoughtful. You are quiet and reserved with deep emotions. You are strong willed and mysterious with the power to regenerate yourself. You can be overly sensitive to the imagined slights of others.

Sagittarius Ascendant

You are an expansive spirit who likes to enjoy life. You are open, outgoing, frank, and honest, expressing your opinions forthrightly. You love the freedom to travel—physically, emotionally, and mentally. You are fearful of being confined.

Capricorn Ascendant

You are a serious spirit who likes to be cautious. You are practical and wish to work hard to achieve things of value. You are organized, competent, and have integrity but can find it difficult to contact your real feelings.

Aquarius Ascendant

You are an individualistic spirit who likes to be gregarious. You want to experience everything that is different and foreign. You have an interest in social reform and in taking up causes. You can be rather too detached, living in your own world.

Pisces Ascendant

You are a sensitive spirit who likes to feel your way through live. You are kind, compassionate, and empathetic, understanding people and tuning in to the vibrations around you. You need a private retreat, as you can lose your way.

THE ASPECTS

The basis of astronomy is the position of the planets with respect to each other and to the stars in the firmament. Like balls on a billiard table, the planets arrange themselves in shifting geometric patterns. For example, at times the Sun, the Moon, and Earth form a triangle; at other times they form a straight line. The angles formed between the various bodies are called *aspects*. Put simply, the energy and influence of an astrological body at any point in its movement rises and falls depending on its aspects in relation to the other bodies. We might say that a planet exerting strong influence over someone's life is *well aspected*.

To grasp the concept, think about the tides. When both the Sun and the Moon are on one side of Earth, their combined gravity produces strong effects on the movements of the waters. But when they're on opposite sides, the gravity of the Moon can strongly counteract the gravity of the Sun. The same types of influences—to greater or lesser degrees—can be ascribed to the aspects of the other planets in a birth chart.

The word *transit* refers to the movements of the planets

at specific times. All astrological bodies are in constant motion. Using transits, an astrologer can determine which planets are moving into which houses or signs. Comparing these movements with the planets' positions in your birth chart can reveal which influences are likely to be felt and to what degree.

CHAPTER 3

The Many Meanings of Mercury

In the last chapter I gave a brief rundown about the effects that the different planets, signs, and Houses have on people. Now it's time to get to the heart of the matter and take a closer look at that speedy little planet called Mercury.

To the ancient romans, Mercury (the Greeks called him Hermes) was the messenger of the gods. Because of his swiftness and eloquence, he was regarded as the god of all forms of communication, governor of the tongue, and guide of intelligent speech.

Mercury had a noble parentage. He was the son of Jupiter (or Zeus, if you're Greek) and a goddess named Maia. His grandfather was Atlas, who carried Earth on his shoulders.

Because of his role as the gods' chief messenger, Mercury had a need for speed. He is usually depicted wearing a winged hat and winged sandals. Perhaps the most famous representation of Mercury in modern times is as the poster boy for FTD, the company that delivers flowers by wire. He also showed up on the "heads" side of U.S. dimes minted between 1916 and 1945. Fittingly, the first manned space flights by U.S. astronauts were part of the Mercury program.

The god Mercury traditionally carried a special symbol, the caduceus. You've probably seen this icon when you visited a doctor's office or hospital: It's the stick that has wings at the top and is entwined with two snakes. The word *caduceus* comes from the Greek word for "herald." Mercury was the herald of the gods. In the old days messengers and ambassadors who carried a caduceus were granted protection—somewhat like carrying a white flag of truce onto the field of battle.

The gods of the ancient world actually had lots of jobs. Mercury was also the god of travelers, and one of his duties was to conduct souls to Hades (the Underworld). He was thought to have magical powers over sleep and dreams. He served as the god of commerce who protected traders and herds of animals. Given his interest in business, he was responsible for inventing astronomy (so ships could navigate to distant ports and deliver their cargoes) and weights and measures (so merchants knew the value of their goods). Since olives and their precious oil were vital to the ancient economy, he developed methods of caring for olive trees. Athletes—especially runners and boxers—prayed and sacrificed to Mercury to grant them luck and victory, and to protect their gyms and stadiums.

Due to his fleet feet and gift of gab, Hermes/Mercury could be a bit of a trickster—and a bit of a thief. (Yes, he's the god of thieves, too—who often wish they had winged feet to make quick getaways!) There are some wonderful stories about the fleet-footed god that reflect his sometimes retrograde nature.

According to legend, on the very day Hermes was born, he stole a herd of cattle from his half brother, the Sun god Apollo. Of course, it isn't easy to hide a herd, and Hermes knew Apollo would track him down. So he fooled his brother by putting shoes on the cows' hooves and making the animals walk backward. Apollo must have admired his kid brother's wily ways, because later they were reconciled. One day he found an object Hermes had invented: a stringed instrument made out of a tortoise shell—the lyre. Apollo demanded the lyre as a token of apology for that little cattle-rustling incident. Hermes is also credited with inventing the pipes and the musical scale. (Surely music can be thought of as one of the most divine ways of communicating ever devised!)

Later, Zeus sent Hermes in his role as messenger to negotiate a pact between two warring kings. Thyestes had used trickery to seize the throne of Mycenae. Atreus, who was favored by the gods, wanted the kingdom for himself. Hermes instructed Atreus to get his rival to agree to a deal: If the Sun should ever run backward in the sky, Thyestes would yield the throne. Believing such a thing could never happen, Thyestes scornfully agreed. But he miscalculated the treacherous power of the gods. As soon as he and Atreus agreed to the deal, the Sun reversed course—and set in the east.

No wonder Mercury Retrograde is associated with so much mischief!

Now let's shift from mythology to astronomy for a

moment for a quick look at the planet Mercury. The closest planet to the Sun (a mere 36 million miles away), it earned its name because it's the fastest of the orbiting bodies. It zips along in its orbit at a speed of 29 miles per second. At this rate it takes only eighty-eight Earth days for Mercury to complete one turn around the Sun. The most distant planet in our solar system, Pluto, moves so slowly that since it was discovered in 1930, it hasn't even traveled halfway across the Zodiac.

Mercury isn't the smallest planet—that honor belongs to Pluto—but it's still only a little bigger than our own Moon. If Earth were the size of a baseball, Mercury would be as big as a golf ball.

You may not want to spend a lot of time there. The Sun would appear three times larger in the sky than it does on Earth, and its bright light would be overpowering. At noon on Mercury, the temperature reaches 700 degrees Fahrenheit. Since the planet has no atmosphere to trap the heat, the temperature falls to 300 degrees below zero at night. (Because Mercury turns so slowly, "noon" can last a couple of days, and night lasts about one Earth month!) Because of its tiny size, its gravity is only about a third of that on Earth.

There's another meaning of the word *mercury*. Spelled with a small m, it's the slippery, silvery, and extremely poisonous metal found in your thermometer. It, too, earned its name because it was associated with the fast-moving god of the Romans. (*Quicksilver*, another name for mercury, means "silver that's alive.") People whose moods change quickly are said to have a "mercurial" personality. In Shakespeare's *Romeo and Juliet* an articulate and hot-tempered character goes by the name Mercutio. He's a great communicator—glib with his tongue, quick with a joke, and no slouch when it comes to lobbing clever insults at his enemies.

THE MR̵ EFFECT AND THE SUN SIGNS

As a player on the astrological stage, the tiny planet Mercury has power over our happiness and well-being—especially in matters of communication. That influence depends on whether Mercury is moving in direct motion or in retrograde. It's also affected by the positions of Mercury in relation to the other planets as expressed in birth charts and horoscopes.

In this chapter we'll explore how Mercury's interaction with your Sun sign affects your ability to communicate. Along the way I'll share stories of the impact that MR̵ has had on people's lives. The next chapter will look at Mercury's influence on the Houses of your birth chart—those areas that represent the different areas of experience and the inner states of your life.

MERCURY AND YOUR HOROSCOPE

What's your personality like? In a group are you sociable, witty, a sparkling conversationalist? Do you love to communicate your ideas? Do you quickly grasp where people are headed with a thought, perhaps jumping in to articulate their conclusion before they get a chance to? Do you finish other people's sentences? Do you love to make a pitch, land the sale, close the deal? If so, it's likely your birth chart has a well-aspected Mercury in direct motion. Or perhaps you're the opposite—quiet, thoughtful, introspective. In that case, there's a good chance Mercury was retrograde when you drew your first breath.

To find out, look up your birth date in the ephemeris (appendix 1). This will tell you whether Mercury was direct or retrograde when you were born, and in what sign of the Zodiac the planet appeared. Then look for your combination in the descriptions below. Here you'll find insights into your personality. You'll also discover stories about how Mercury impacts people's lives.

Please bear in mind that the following material is only a general guide to certain information revealed by your birth chart or your horoscope. The aspects of other planets can modify these descriptions to a greater or lesser degree. Also, the exact time and location of your birth makes a big difference in the positions of planets. A person born at 12:01 A.M. in Nome, Alaska, will have a significantly different chart than someone born the same day at 11:59 P.M. in Key West, Florida. For information on how to obtain a more complete and accurate reading, see Resources at the end of the book.

MERCURY DIRECT

In astrological terms, Mercury represents the messenger. The way you communicate depends on the aspects of Mercury in relationship with the other bodies, as expressed in your birth chart. At its best, Mercury serves as the channel that conveys wisdom from your higher self. You may perceive such messages as a flash of insight or intuition, a noble thought, or a heroic decision. At worst, Mercury is the purveyor of gossip and trivia.

Mercury governs the mind and all the ways the mind expresses itself in the world—its logical and reasoning capabilities. That's why Mercury is so closely tied with communication. It represents the drive and energy that motivate you to speak, write, dance, and sing. It is your intrinsic brightness and the light in your eyes, the ever-changing consciousness within you that moves from thought to thought, idea to idea.

In the physical body Mercury is associated with the nervous system—appropriate, given that the nerves carry electrical signals to and from the brain, literally at lightning speed. By extension, Mercury is involved with travel (especially the day-to-day kind), transportation, and movement. Such activities require good, clear communication to function properly.

Mercury governs such basic human activities as the formation of ideas and their expression in words or symbols: maps, charts, images, musical notation, lines of computer code. We use such symbols as a way of preserving and sharing information about ourselves and our world. Thus Mercury is a primary force underlying the creation of culture, its expression, its memory, and its transmission. The power of Mercury allows us to bridge gaps—between people, between places, between ideas.

People who possess a mercurial nature tend to be restless, eager for new stimulation. The downside is that they might want to move on to the next event before they've had time to digest what's happened.

Mercury is concerned with details. (If your job is to be the messenger of the gods, you'd better be sure you get the message right!) The downside of this is that it can lead to an overemphasis on the specifics of things at the expense of the "big picture." People with strong mercurial personalities might have trouble seeing the forest for the trees.

In broad strokes, people whose birth charts show Mercury direct, especially a Mercury that is well aspected with other bodies, are able to express themselves well in speech or writing. They are logical and can memorize quickly— they're famous for being "quick studies." A good many authors, scientists, inventors, journalists, and singers have strong Mercury influences. So do sharp deal makers and traders.

MERCURY RETROGRADE

Planetary retrograde motion is actually an illusion. The planets never reverse course and travel backward. They only appear to do so from our perspective on Earth. Let me explain.

We humans detect that something is moving by comparing it to objects that are relatively stationary. If you're standing on a street corner and a car passes by, you can easily see that it's moving because everything else around you—the buildings, the traffic lights, the pavement beneath your feet—is standing still. (We can ignore the fact that Earth itself is hurtling through space at more than a thousand miles an hour, because—thanks to gravity!—everything attached to the planet is moving at exactly the same speed. That's what I mean when I say something is "relatively" stationary.)

The picture changes considerably when both the object and the observer are in motion. Imagine that you're driving in one car, moving in the same direction as another car on your left. If the two cars are moving at different speeds, one will gradually fall behind the other. A car might be racing forward at 60 miles an hour, but from your perspective, riding in a car doing 65, the other car is moving backward at a rate of 5 miles per hour. That's one way to understand the concept of retrograde motion—it's an illusion based on a trick of perspective and relative motion.

But this analogy is not completely accurate when it comes to describing the planets. For one thing, both planets orbit at constant (and different) speeds. Earth actually moves more slowly in its orbit than Mercury— about 18 miles per second, compared to Mercury's 29 miles per second. Instead, to understand retrograde, we need to think of the motions of the planets as a ballet that takes place against a backdrop of stars—the Zodiac.

Imagine that you're watching a dance performance at a theater. At the back of the stage, as part of the scenery, there's an immense painting divided into three sections. Each section contains a different image: a pair of twins on the left, a bull in the center, and a ram on the right.

Sitting in the center of the audience, you see a dancer standing at the edge of the stage to your left. He begins to move in a circle, going counterclockwise. In this circle he first moves downstage, toward you, then upstage, away from you. From your angle, he begins his circle while positioned in front of the image of the twins. As he moves, you see him pass in front of the bull, then the ram. Having completed half the circle, he turns and completes the second half of the circle. Moving upstage, he passes in front of the ram, then the bull. At the end of his circle he stands once again before the twins.

Now let's replay the scene, but this time you're in a theater that has no seats—just an open floor that allows you to move about easily.

Imagine that you are now standing not in the center but at the far left of the floor. From your perspective, a dancer stands before the painting of the twins. As she begins to trace the same circle, you too begin moving to your right. Like a moving camera tracking her motion, you never take your eyes off her. By the time she's completed half the circle, you're both now standing all the way to the right of the stage. From this extreme angle, the dancer no longer appears to be standing in front of the ram. Instead she's in front of the bull, the image in the center of the backdrop. At some point, as you moved in your path and she moved in hers, she appeared to move backward for a short time— *but only in relationship to the painting behind her.*

The "dancer" in this little ballet is Mercury, and the "audience" is Earth. The backdrop contains some of the signs of the Zodiac: Gemini, Taurus, and Aries. The illusion of a backward motion is the retrograde period.

All the planets display retrograde motion (relative to Earth) at some point in their orbits. When the planet moves forward, we call this *direct* motion. When the planet appears to stop moving forward, we say that it *stations* (that is, it becomes stationary). At the end of retrograde, the planet stations and then begins direct motion again. Retrograde can occur only when the planet is closest to Earth—that is, when it's on the same side of the Sun as we are, moving in the same direction. Because the planets are closer during these times, their influence on us tends to be greater.

As a rule, people have several retrograde planets in their birth charts. During retrograde, the influence of the planet tends to become the opposite of what it is normally. For example, Mars is the planet associated with physical strength. During Mars retrograde, therefore, we may feel weak, tired, and lethargic. On a more positive level, the "backward" influence of the energies may assist us to be more introspective.

MR℞

Retrograde planets in your birth chart (and most of us have two or more) can mean that the particular energy represented by the planet may not be expressed easily or openly. Often a retrograde motion suggests that the opposite form of the planet's energy will be made manifest. People with many retrograde planets have a certain mystery about them. They may be reluctant to reveal themselves, or they may be shy. By the same token, people with no retrograde planets can be overwhelmingly direct, almost confrontational in nature.

Mercury Retrograde in your chart can mean broken or

thwarted lines of communication. M℞ or a badly aspected Mercury is associated with speech impediments, leaky memory, and slow thinking. Reading can be hard for people born during M℞; they may instead be more visually or physically inclined.

But some people who are born during M℞ feel quite at home when things are going backward. For example, if you began reading this book by flipping through the pages from back to front, I suspect you have M℞ in your birth chart. I know an in-line skater who has developed her special ability to skate backward. A friend of mind who has strong M℞ says he likes to read the end of a detective novel to find out "whodunit," then read the story from the beginning to trace how the plot unfolds.

Many scientists, architects, and moviemakers are born under the influence of M℞, which they manifest in their ability to envision a goal—a great experiment, a magnificent building, a classic film—and then work backward step by step to achieve their dream. Clearly, far from being a handicap, M℞ gives them a special knack of looking at life from a different perspective and expressing themselves in unusual and creative ways. They are inventive and often quicker to see how things will turn out in the end. At times, however, they may overlook the obvious or appear to be slow. They're not—they just tend to reflect on information before assimilating it. Because most people around them are moving in the other direction, as it were, people born under M℞ may lack self-confidence and may be too willing to defer to others.

As the patron of alchemy, Mercury inspired ancient scientists to experiment with converting one substance into another. (Indeed, in the field of mining, the element mercury is used to extract gold from crushed ore.) If you understand MR̥, you can become an alchemist of sorts, using the power of Mercury to transform base thoughts into higher forms of insight and intuition. Seen from the proper perspective, the disruptions of communication during MR̥ periods are in fact wonderful gifts—the opportunity to learn to review, reflect on, and reconsider steps you've taken. More about this later.

In the following chapter I'll explain how people with different Sun signs are affected by periods of Mercury Retrograde.

CHAPTER 4

Mercury and the Signs of the Zodiac

Now let's explore the influence of Mercury on each of the signs of the Zodiac, from Aries to Pisces. In your birth chart you will discover that, although Mercury is near your Sun sign, it may be in a different sign of the Zodiac. For example, I have an Aries Sun, but my "Mercury sign" is in the following sign of Taurus. My husband, also an Aries Sun sign, has his natal Mercury in Aries, and a good friend of mine, who is yet another Aries (we stick together!), has Mercury in the preceding sign of Pisces. Although we each approach life in a similar way, we think and express ourselves very differently.

As well as knowing your Sun sign, it is therefore helpful for you also to know your Mercury sign. (To find your Mercury sign, please refer to appendix 1.) Because Mercury in your birth chart relates to your mental development, the way you communicate, and the expression of your innate intelligence, understanding more about your Mercury sign is as valuable as assessing the qualities of your Sun sign, Moon sign, or Ascendant.

There is yet another Mercury factor to consider. Was the speedy planet Mercury traveling forward or was it doing its backward dance at the time you were born? (Again, refer to appendix 1 to find out if your natal Mercury is direct or retrograde.) It will affect how you communicate and express yourself now.

Armed with information about your Mercury sign, read the following section. You will see how Mercury is colored by the qualities of the particular sign of the Zodiac it is in. Also, you will see the difference between having Mercury Direct in your birth chart and Mercury Retrograde. Finally, you will see how your particular Sun sign fares during periods of Mercury Retrograde and how you can make the best of these times.

ARIES

Aries is the first sign of the Zodiac. As an Aries, you're often the leader of the pack—an initiator, someone who possesses a pioneering, adventurous, and enterprising nature. Honest and to the point, you may be unusually courageous, self-assertive, and dynamic. On the downside, you can also be selfish, impatient, and quarrelsome. An impulsive sort, you may prefer starting projects to actually completing them.

Mercury Direct in Aries

The presence of Mercury Direct in Aries suggests you communicate with others in a strong, self-assertive manner.

You are a person who thrives on challenge. While other people seek harmony and peace, you enjoy the stimulation of an argument or heated debate. Nothing is more boring to you than to be surrounded by complacent people with no opinions. You can think on your feet and excel in debate, but you may become resentful or impatient with others if they are slower than you are (which most of us are). You're quick to get to the essence of a thing and can see through gobbledygook. You do not suffer fools gladly and can be irritable when dealing with people of a more sensitive nature.

Perceptive and intuitive, you are often a step (or many steps) ahead of others, which can be frustrating for you and annoying for them. Fortunately, your leadership ability, quick wit, and original, decisive mind often help you find environments (work, relationships, family life) that support your unique skills.

MR℞ in Aries

Your mind is just as keen and sharp as Mercury Direct in Aries, but it operates differently. You can be easily distracted by new ideas and lack patience. Because of this you may appear abrupt and slightly out of sync with what's going on. You respond to the subconscious motivations of others rather than to what they are actually saying. You may be misunderstood, and your laserlike focus can be extremely uncomfortable for others. Take a deep breath and listen to what they're actually saying rather than to what you *think* they're saying.

It is especially important for you to understand others and forgive their weaknesses. Realize that communication is a two-way process. Yes, of course, you need to express yourself. Bear in mind, however, that what you say has the power to hurt and wound. You are responsible for the effect of your words. Be careful not to say things that can come back to hurt you!

If you turn your mind inward and become more controlled in your speech and actions, you can be a tremendous power for good and an inspirational leader. You have the power to regenerate yourself through this process of self-analysis in a way that few people can. This power also enables you to renew your health and your life spirit so that others may see you as eternally youthful.

How Aries Survives During Mercury Retrograde

Frank is the type of guy you go to when you want to get things done. He's an Aries—eager to lead, bursting with creativity. An account exec with an advertising agency, he's earned a reputation as someone who can pick up the phone and within a few minutes land a new account. What's more, he's usually the one who comes up with the initial concepts for ad campaigns. His head explodes with so many ideas that people call him Pop—short for "popcorn."

But during MR Frank says he feels more like an "old maid"—an unpopped kernel of corn lying forlornly in the bottom of the bowl. During retrograde periods his creative energy wanes. Those ideas just don't come. And communication grinds to a halt. "I seem to be caught in an endless round of telephone tag," he says. "I keep missing people, messages don't get delivered. When we do talk, it's as if we have a bad connection."

Once he learned about the M℞ effect, though, Frank discovered how he could turn it to his advantage. Rather than chasing new business, Frank takes the time during M℞ to review the status of current accounts. His clients say they appreciate knowing that he stays so involved with them. He doesn't worry if new ideas are slow to come. Instead, he's found that what he calls the "creative cortex" of his brain remains active in the background, even if he isn't consciously aware of it. He often schedules vacations or "personal days" during M℞. Once Mercury goes direct again, so does Frank—in a flurry of phone calls and a renewed surge of creativity.

Aries Mercury Retrograde Survival Tips

- Put a temporary stopper on new ideas and use the time to constructively review things that are already under way.
- Count to three before making those split-second decisions you are normally so good at.
- Take some of that unused vacation time and relax.
- Do a kind deed for someone else.

TAURUS

Taurus is symbolized by the bull—an animal of great strength and power that wears horns in the shape of a crescent Moon. This symbolizes the wisdom and truth that need to be manifested in the world. In the Zodiac, Taurus is sometimes called the maintainer.

As a Taurus, you have a desire for solid ground. You tend to be calm and steadfast—perhaps a bit stodgy at times. You are persistent, the type who knows how to bring other people's flashes of inspiration to fruition. Often possessed of a feel for money and business, many people born in Taurus also use their keen senses to become art lovers, gourmets, and healers. On the downside, you can be bullheaded, with a stubborn streak that makes you possessive or unyielding. If you don't get your way, there's a chance you'll practice a little passive aggression, becoming lethargic, perhaps a little lazy.

Mercury Direct in Taurus

Like other people with Mercury in Taurus, you probably don't put up with—excuse the expression—bull. But like the proverbial bull in the china shop, you need to tread carefully. You may see the truth, but you may need to learn to speak it with kindness and patience.

You possess a rare gift: common sense, which today isn't so common! You have a patient, practical, and possessive mind, with outstanding powers of concentration. Your thinking tends to be conservative and your thought processes fixed and stable (some may even say stubborn). You do not like to be pushed into making decisions, because you prefer to give a question a lot of thought before rendering your answer. Your opinions—heartfelt and strong—may be too much for weaker souls.

You have a shrewd business mind; people cannot easily fool you or pull the wool over your eyes. You are good at handling money and resources in general. You have an innate understanding of life, and you have a genius for bringing your ideals and values to fruition. Once you make up your mind, however, you don't like to change it, even if you turn out to be wrong.

MR in Taurus

You tend to constantly question your values and resources and compare them to what others have. Doing so helps you find greater stability and security in your own life, but is ultimately a waste of your time and energy. Instead, you'd be better served using this inner reflection to reassess your values from time to time.

You have a tendency to hold on to things that you have outgrown, and you can fixate on a thought until it becomes an obsession. These traits can block you from being the person you want to be. Try concentrating on becoming more open and understanding of others rather than holding on to dead-end thoughts and petty prejudices. Assess and weigh the things that provide real and lasting value in your life. As you do, you'll rid yourself of prejudices that weigh you down.

You often have fears about money and security. Such fears do not serve you. If you can dispel these fears, you're more likely to find the success and stability necessary to nurture the growth of your soul.

How Taurus Survives
During Mercury Retrograde

Ever since he was a kid, Nick has loved cars. At the age of three, Nick, a Taurus, figured out how to take apart his toy fire truck and put it back together (with most of the pieces in the right place!). In high school he spent most Saturday afternoons in the garage, keeping his dad's car as well tuned as a Stradivarius violin. His dad paid him the ultimate compliment: "This car hums at a perfect pitch!"

Not surprisingly, Nick went into the auto repair business. His shop does a thriving business. But he noticed there were times when things didn't go so well. His diagnostic machine would go on the fritz or register false data. Customers seemed to have more trouble than usual describing the problem: "It kinda goes 'chunka-chunka ping'—know what I mean?" His auto parts dealer would run out of the very parts he needed to complete a job. But the worst was when a repair he made failed, causing a car to crash. Fortunately, no one was hurt—but Nick had to pay such a big settlement that he was almost forced to close up shop. Looking back over his business records one night, Nick discovered that these problems seemed to come in clusters—during periods of MR.

After talking to an astrologer, Nick realized there were ways he could minimize the fallout during retrograde. He now schedules big jobs for these periods—rebuilding engines, large-scale body repair problems. This way he minimizes the number of customers he deals with and the need for rushed emergency work. He can also order parts far in advance to reduce the chance of running into stock shortages. When possible, he closes the shop to take care of bookkeeping, inventory, or other nonmechanical tasks. And he orders all his workers, including himself, to triple-check their work before sending a car back on the road— not just during M℞, but at all times.

Taurus Mercury Retrograde Survival Tips

- Keep your investments safe and secure: It's not the time to play the markets.
- Minimize business problems by planning and ordering in advance.
- Visit an art gallery and spend time with your favorite paintings.
- Cook a special celebration meal for someone who needs cheering up.

GEMINI

As a Gemini, you are a questioner. You display a deep curiosity about the way things work. On the highest level, you are a constant seeker of truth. You are rational and artic-ulate (if a little wordy) in your dealings with others. A dex-terous type, you are likely to enjoy working with your hands. At times your curiosity and imagination may get the better of you. You're the type who might push that little red button marked DON'T TOUCH!—just to see what happens. You're flexible, able to try a lot of different approaches to prob-lems—in some ways, a jack-of-all-trades.

On the downside, you tend to bounce from one thing to another without settling on one for too long. Others might see you as frivolous, fickle, nervous, or a bit too willing to bend the facts to suit your needs.

Mercury Direct in Gemini

Mercury rules the sign of Gemini and feels at home here. If you have Mercury Direct in Gemini, you are quick thinking, intelligent, talkative, and witty. You love logic and rational thought. You can be an excellent teacher, since you enjoy facts and appreciate subjects such as mathematics and language.

You excel in arguments. Your opponents can be won over by your rational remarks; they may not even notice that you sometimes misrepresent a basic premise or two. You are very curious and ask lots of questions but rarely look beneath the surface for the answers.

You have the ability to see many sides of every issue—and this can make choices difficult. You also have a tendency to spread yourself too thin, which can create stress, especially with the sensitive nervous system you have. It is essential that you take frequent breaks so you can recharge your batteries.

MR in Gemini

When retrograde, the fast energies of Mercury in Gemini slow down. Your inquisitiveness risks being transformed into indecisiveness, since you explore every side of a question and struggle to reach a conclusion. On the other hand, this shift in energy can work to your advantage. You might become more thorough, delving deeper into subconscious factors and motivations.

Your mind is often full of a thousand different dilemmas, which you see as puzzles to be solved. During MR you might actually focus long enough to solve some of them! You are inquisitive and adept at complex verbal manipulations. One of your greatest strengths is that you are a lifelong student, always eager to learn.

It is important that you use your mind as a tool, rather than letting your mind use you. You are likely to find inner peace through meditation techniques, trips into nature, and creative pursuits. All of these can serve to slow down the pace of your overactive mind and help you reconcile opposing thoughts into positive, productive courses of action.

How Gemini Survives During
Mercury Retrograde

Paula, a Gemini, works in a pathology lab. Peering through a microscope, she analyzes medical samples to detect signs of disease. She's highly respected for her ability to discern subtle clues to a patient's problem. As she explains it, that's because she doesn't take anything for granted. No matter what the preliminary report accompanying the sample says, Paula asks her own tough, unbiased questions.

She's recently noticed, however, that during MR she has more trouble coming up with a definitive diagnosis. "It's as if the lens on my scope is cloudy or scratched," she says. The lab reports she writes during these times are usually correct, but they have an annoying tendency to get lost in the shuffle. Since lives literally depend on her ability to analyze samples accurately and submit reports to doctors in a timely fashion, she was naturally pretty worried about the problem.

After learning about what can happen during retrograde periods, though, Paula developed strategies for coping. She frequently asks a coworker to double-check her findings. She makes it a point to follow up with her managers to be sure that reports are delivered on time. She also schedules plenty of "downtime" to clean and maintain her instruments.

Gemini Mercury Retrograde Survival Tips

- Don't trust your own analyses; double-check your findings and think twice before making decisions.
- Take time out to clean your computer and all your equipment.
- Read that novel you have been promising yourself for the past year.
- Speak kindly to everyone you meet.

CANCER

Cancer is considered the nurturer of the Zodiac. If you were born with the Sun in Cancer, you are likely to be sensitive, tender, concerned, and sympathetic to others' needs.

You are a wonderful protector—of people, ideas, and concepts. Many Cancers are fiercely patriotic, loyal to a fault, and sensitive and intuitive about people's deeper feelings. Typically Cancers find careers as teachers, parents, and politicians, where they can nurture people and causes. With their retentive memories, they make fine public speakers.

On the downside, Cancers can be manipulative and insecure, often wondering why others with different Sun signs don't express the same nurturing qualities toward them. The symbol of Cancer is the crab—and watch out for those pincers! They can hold on to things a little too tightly. The wisdom expressed by this Zodiacal image is to hold on to that which is precious and let go of the rest.

Mercury Direct in Cancer

While people with Mercury in Gemini tend to be logical, those with Mercury in Cancer are more likely to be intuitive. When confronting a problem, you may find it difficult to be objective since you are influenced more by an appeal to your senses or by your "gut feeling" than by logic. You have an excellent memory and can recall things, places, people, and events clearly and in great detail. You generally have a love for family, tradition, history, and your roots.

Because you are very sensitive and empathetic to other people, you can be vulnerable. You should discriminate carefully when choosing to spend time with people. Otherwise you risk giving away too much of your time and energy to others who may not value your gifts as highly as they should.

MR in Cancer

You have an inward-looking mind dominated by your feelings. Your tendency is to evaluate ideas to see if they make you feel secure. In forming relationships, you look for independence of thought and emotional security at the same time.

It is very difficult for you to let go of the past. As a highly sensitive creature, you may need to make more of an effort to retreat into your shell, reassess your situation, clear away baggage from the past, and reinvent yourself.

You have the ability to reach others through your speaking and writing because you can touch people deeply at the level of their feelings. Possessed of unusual charm, you can be loving, kind and sympathetic, and have a wonderful rapport with children.

How Cancer Survives During
Mercury Retrograde

A former history teacher of mine, Kathy, has Mercury in Cancer. She was a great listener, and lots of us were instinctively drawn to her to discuss our worries. She not only listened to what we said, but also really seemed to care. She was a universal mother figure to all of us—students and friends alike.

She also had a photographic memory and could remember facts and figures from the past, as well as the name of your latest boyfriend and all the important stuff. A bit of a showman, she liked to make us laugh.

Then one day—it happened to be during a time of MR—she didn't show up for class. For weeks no one was quite sure what had happened. Eventually we learned that she had taken a leave of absence, escaping to the peace and quiet of the countryside. She had expended so much energy nurturing others that she had depleted her own reserves.

Like many other Cancers, Kathy had a gift for caring for others—but she had neglected to take care of her own needs. Over the years we've stayed in touch, and I've shared with her what I've learned about MR. Now she plans ahead to make sure that during these periods she also takes care of herself. As she told me, "When I left school that time, I felt guilty for being so selfish. Now I realize that if I give myself the loving care I need, I'm better able to care for others. In the end, that's not really selfish, is it?"

Cancer Mercury Retrograde Survival Tips

- Take time out to listen to your own needs.
- Recall all the good things and people in your life, and allow this daily reflection to nurture and uplift you.
- Have a massage and enjoy yourself.
- Nurture someone who needs your help; tell a story and make others laugh.

LEO

Like their symbol, the lion, people whose Sun sign is Leo can be bold, regal, strong, and self-confident. Kings of the realm, they are able to see the big picture. They inspire trust in others and can lead with benevolence, dignity, and honor. They have a flair for the dramatic and enjoy being the focus of attention. Warm and generous, their strength of purpose allows them to accomplish a great deal.

Of course, there's a downside to all this. Without other qualities to balance them, Leos can be arrogant, egocentric, and downright domineering. It doesn't take much to push a "king" over the edge into being a "dictator." That dramatic flair? In the extreme it becomes ostentation and pomposity.

Mercury Direct in Leo

You have a positive outlook with strong willpower. You can see the larger picture, but you can be rather fixed in your opinions. Despite what others may say, you just know you're right! (And often, darn it, you are.) You're the "big-picture" person, preferring to let others handle the details for you.

You usually make decisions that most people can accept. Because of this, you often find yourself in a leadership position—a position that you like and that feels natural to you. You know how to present yourself with confidence and a demeanor that commands respect. Your innate sense of authority is aided by a natural flair for generous gestures.

It's important for you to be "lion minded" as well as "lionhearted." Be on guard against your tendency to swagger, to impose your will on others. Before handing down your decisions, take the time to explore your heart to know that you're following a proper path.

MR. in Leo

You are a person who can reflect on your own insights and enjoy your own creativity. You can be your own audience and even supply your own applause! You can also, however, be mentally lazy and resistant to change. As a result, you may tend to talk about what you want to achieve rather than do it.

If you can keep your tendency to exaggerate in check, you can be exceptionally creative. You are able, through examining your own motivations, to motivate, inspire, and uplift the hearts of others. You can also help others see a clearer vision of the whole, while they are only able to catch glimpses.

How Leo Survives During Mercury Retrograde

Tamara is an actress enjoying a budding career in Los Angeles. She came here a few years ago at the encouragement of her parents, who recognized early on that she had a flair for the dramatic. A gifted mimic with the singing voice of a pint-sized Ethel Merman, Tamara entertained family at holiday gatherings and would often disrupt class with her antics. After arriving in Hollywood, she landed a string of bit parts in movies and some recurring roles in TV soap operas. "All I have to do is keep twinkling, and one day I'll be a star," she likes to say.

Acting is a tough row to hoe, but Tamara has told me that it's particularly tough during MR̥. Agents don't return phone calls. Auditions get canceled. "Shooting schedules basically go kaflooie," she says. During one recent retrograde she ordered new photographs of herself—and when they came back from the shop, they were printed in reverse and upside down.

As part of her survival skills, Tamara has learned to lower expectations during MR̥. "That's when I'm more inclined to accept a 'lead role' as a temporary waitress," she wisecracks. She makes sure to send out résumés before or after MR̥. She's also put her agent on notice not to schedule auditions during these periods. "Of course, if Steven Spielberg ever calls, put him through," she says. "I don't care if Mercury crashes into my bedroom that day— put him through!"

Leo Mercury Retrograde Survival Tips

- Check that the tickets for the play you are in were mailed—or you may be without an audience!
- Keep up your daily gym workouts—but don't skip the warm-up.
- Don't hire a new managing director for your company just yet. Instead, review the candidates' backgrounds carefully—and wait.
- Be generous to all you meet.

VIRGO

Ever practical, ever analytical, Virgos are the efficiency experts of the Zodiac. Others may dream, others may plan—Virgos get things done. In a way, the traits of a Virgo read like the Boy Scout Law: trustworthy, loyal, helpful . . . People born with the Sun in Virgo are industrious, methodical, efficient, and possessed of a strong sense of duty. Detail-oriented, conscientious, they make good engineers, secretaries, or civic personnel.

Of course, in extreme cases Virgos can be hypercritical or intolerant. Their focus on detail can make them tedious or superficial. They don't just *collect*—they *obsess* over their collection. If things aren't perfect—plans, circumstances—Virgos can be miserable. In some cases, if they experience less-than-ideal health, they can tend to be a bit neurotic, even hypochondriacal.

Mercury Direct in Virgo

You have a practical, logical, critical mind. You are aware of the importance of precision and detail. Because of your inclination to dot the i's and cross the t's, you can be successful with any task you undertake. Your mind is discriminating, but you can get so caught up in the details that you sometimes can't see the forest for the trees.

Your environment affects your mind more than most. For this reason, it's important for you to work and live in an orderly environment. You crave routines and are likely to set up systems that improve not only your environment, home, office, and garden but also your own physical health. You're hardworking and appreciate the value of education and of learning new technical skills. Despite this, you often lack confidence in yourself. Sometimes you hesitate before acting in order to check and recheck your decisions. If you're not careful, you can fall victim to "analysis paralysis."

MR in Virgo

You analyze everything you see, feel, and perceive. Because of this, you can be rather strict with yourself and others, and can exhibit little tolerance for disorder. As a strong objective thinker, you are good at solving problems. But you tend to be opinionated about how others should live, which keeps you at a slight distance from them—by both your choice and theirs.

You have lots of internal checklists for everything—from the things you want to achieve to what you are feeling! You tend to categorize everything but sometimes do it in an unusual way so that only you can understand your system. You may even drive yourself to distraction with your constant analysis.

How Virgo Survives During Mercury Retrograde

Andrea impressed people with her intelligence and efficiency. She was constantly on the go. Besides holding down a full-time job as a town council administrator, she also served on several voluntary committees. Not content to attend the meetings herself, she often picked people up to make sure they were there on time. Always punctual and reliable, she was the one who would take the minutes, bake the cookies, and clean up afterward. Everyone relied upon her quiet efficiency.

Until . . . until MR struck, and with a vengeance. "My life fell apart," Andrea recalled some years later. "I was racing to some meeting or other. I didn't see a stop sign and got in a bad wreck. I was carrying money from the committee treasury—it was more than a thousand dollars—and somebody stole it from the car while it was being towed. People accused me of embezzling! In the accident I broke two fingers and so I couldn't use the computer for weeks. I got so far behind in my work I just about had a nervous breakdown."

Andrea abruptly resigned her many posts. Her plan, she said, was to move to the countryside and look after her garden, her two cats—and herself. Privately she confided to friends that she didn't want to wait on anyone else ever again. Everyone was stunned and shocked. Then they realized how much they had taken her for granted. They had not noticed her poor health. Some realized they had never thanked her adequately for her support and hard work.

But after a year of retirement, Andrea was back. During her sabbatical she found a new understanding. She realized she did not have to wait on people who could easily wait on themselves. Instead, she devoted her volunteer energies to working among the sick and elderly. She telephoned shut-ins and visited hospitals and hospices, where she brightened the days of the terminally ill with her stories and expressions of concern.

Andrea told me that surviving her encounter with MR had taught her a valuable lesson: to use her time more discriminately. She had previously encouraged others to lean on her, making them weak and herself even weaker. Now she was giving strength to those who really needed her help. This in turn regenerated her strength and compassion. As she put it, she had learned how to "do God's work."

Virgo Mercury Retrograde Survival Tips

- Streamline your life, do all your filing, and get organized.
- Say no when asked to help in yet another project, unless it's really essential.
- Feeling frazzled?—take time out to have a guilt-free relaxing day.
- Lend a helping hand to someone who really needs it.

LIBRA

Looking to name an ambassador to handle tricky negotiations? Need someone to render an impartial verdict to help you resolve a conflict? Consider asking a Libra. Like their symbol, the scales, Libras are adept at striking the right balance. They are thoughtful, considerate, and diplomatic. They can take the needs of many people into account and find a harmonious solution that works (for the majority, anyway). Masters of fair play and square deals, Libras are the judges of the Zodiac, objective in their approach, wanting the best outcome for everyone.

At the other end of the spectrum, people born with the Sun in Libra may tend to weigh so many options that they are unable to make a judgment call. They can seem critical or argumentative because of their devotion to leaving no stone unturned. They value objectivity, and so at times seem distant or cold. Because so many people value their opinions, they sometimes appear arrogant or conceited.

Mercury Direct in Libra

Your Libran mentality wants harmony and justice. You appear polished and prefer reason and debate to argument. You enjoy people and will be sought out for all kinds of social events. You enjoy learning about people and can listen with interest and reply honestly and fairly. If you find yourself caught in the middle of conflict, however, you would rather back away and leave the matter to more aggressive characters. To you, harmony is essential at all costs.

You are at your best in a position of mediator, where you can relate fully to two distinct sides of an issue. You tend to see the good in both sides and therefore may have difficulty in making decisions. Justice is important, however, and you will strive to weigh both sides to come to a just solution.

MR in Libra

You weigh everything you see and hear but tend to believe that everyone is basically the same underneath. At times, then, you may lack discrimination or render superficial judgments. You tend to be indecisive because of this, so that even people who are close to you do not understand where you are coming from. For the sake of harmony, you sometimes go along with the opinions of the people you're with, whether or not you feel those opinions are correct. Others may come to mistrust your judgment.

How Libra Survives During
Mercury Retrograde

Peter has Mercury in Libra and, true to form, he's an attorney who enjoys the challenge of the courtroom. He's proud of his dedication to justice, and his clients feel well represented whenever he goes to bat for them before the judge.

Most of the time Peter is organized and efficient. He can whip together a powerful courtroom argument on a moment's notice, complete with case citations and methodically written briefs. He skewers witnesses with his pointed cross-examinations or sways sullen juries with his impassioned summations.

Ah, but there is no law that prevents MR from wreaking havoc, even for an attorney sworn to defend the public good. A few years ago Peter recognized that during these periods he can fumble as badly as a novice lawyer fighting his first client's parking ticket. Important documents go astray. Legal research hits blind alleys. "What's worse," he says, "every one of my objections is overruled. I feel like the gods are conspiring against me."

I pointed out to him that it wasn't the gods, it was just one—Mercury. And it wasn't a conspiracy, it was simply a force of nature.

Fortunately, Peter says, he realized there were things he could do to minimize the damage. Whenever possible, he avoids scheduling court appearances during M℞. He hires clerks and paralegals on a temporary basis to help him prepare documents. He won't accept new clients or cases during these times, just to reduce the chances that communication will break down. And he devotes extra time to details. Now, he says, if a verdict goes against him during M℞, "at least I know I've lost on the merits of the case and not because the planets were misaligned."

Libra Mercury Retrograde Survival Tips

- Don't enter into any contracts. If you must, have the contract double-checked before you sign it.
- Visit old friends rather than seeking new ones.
- Be the peacemaker but don't compromise yourself to do so. Keep your own life as harmonious as possible.
- Meditate. Keep yourself balanced by exercising your spiritual as well as your physical self.

SCORPIO

Scorpios are serious in their mission to learn about life. They will zero in on essential questions, gleaning the secrets that lie within. They are secretive but also love to dig deep. They are intuitive, intense, resourceful, and passionate. As the catalysts of the Zodiac, Scorpios are frequently effective agents of great change—yet somehow they manage to escape being changed themselves in the process. Given their ability to see beyond the surface, they often make adept investigators. Their ability to transform bad into good makes them excellent doctors, healers, and scientists.

But like their namesakes, Scorpios can sting. They often suppress their emotions, releasing them in a furious explosion. They can sense when people are concealing something from them, and that stirs their anger. Sometimes they use their insight into people's thoughts to manipulate them for their own selfish ends. There's seldom any middle ground with a Scorpio; things are all one way or another, all black or all white.

Mercury Direct in Scorpio

You have a highly intuitive mind that can reach the heart of a problem or a person quickly and easily. You can sense the motives behind the words of people and act like a detective in getting to the bottom of complex issues. You express yourself positively, though you can be rather intolerant and critical of others if you believe they're superficial. You are a deep thinker who searches for meaning and the deeper issues of our existence.

It is important for you to realize that your mind is a tool to assist you through life, not life itself. You can then use it to cope with crises. First, realize that you face tests and conflicts more frequently than most people, and that these moments offer opportunities for growth. Don't approach your tests with passive resistance—instead confront them directly with all the courage and conviction you possess. Death and rebirth are associated with Scorpio. Like the phoenix rising from the fire, you can emerge triumphant from the hardest tests; the base metal of your nature can be turned to pure gold.

You are quite secretive, and because of this others are drawn to unload their own secrets on you, or through you. They instinctively feel their secrets are safe with you. True, you can be silent, but when the mood strikes, you can be sharp tongued, lashing out with your incisive insights, disregarding the feelings of others. You can be blinded by prejudice favoring your own stubborn opinions, which you base on feelings and insights, rather than on objective reality. That's not to say you're wrong—often you're irritatingly right! But unless you're careful you may alienate others, rather than persuading them that you're on the right track.

MR in Scorpio

You have the ability to see deep within other people and discover their true motives and subconscious desires. You are also very idealistic. This combination can make you very critical of others—and you may also find negative thoughts repeating themselves in your mind endlessly. You are never satisfied with superficial explanations and may prefer to live in a world of fantasy. This world can be much more fulfilling than the real world you see around you. The trick, however, is to realize it is just a fantasy.

You also have the power to face your own inner demons and transmute them. Suspicious by nature, you are at your best when focused spiritually. At such moments you develop great inner strength and individuality, which enable you to overcome setbacks and difficulties.

How Scorpio Survives During
Mercury Retrograde

Louisa has been a pharmacist for more than twenty years. She has the extraordinary gift of being able to discern what's ailing her customers as soon as they enter the store. From the look of pain in their eyes or the shuffle of their walk, she senses what's wrong and is able to point them to the shelf that contains the most likely remedy.

In addition to filling prescriptions, Louisa carries a full line of natural herbs and vitamins. She also sells books about healing practices. One day she was flipping through an astrology book and discovered the principle of Mercury Retrograde. A light dawned on her. There were periods of time, she realized, that MR seemed to have an impact on her practice. She remembered a series of episodes not too long ago in which she came close to filling prescriptions incorrectly. At first she blamed the doctors' lousy hand-writing, or the confusing and sound-alike names of some drugs. But then she realized that for a few weeks each year communication just seemed harder, more disrupted than usual. Given her role as a dispenser of potent medications, she knew she had to take some action.

During Mercury Retrograde Louisa implemented a policy requiring everyone on her staff to call the doctor's office and confirm the prescription—drug name, dosage, everything. She cross-checks that the pills she's dispensing exactly match their descriptions in the manual. And she hired high school kids to go through her inventory three times a year and look for products whose expiration dates have passed. "Take no chances" is the new staff motto.

Scorpio Mercury Retrograde Survival Tips

- Don't bottle up or boil over; channel your natural inten-sity through swimming, yoga, or tai chi.
- Slow down and meditate; find answers to the meaning of life.
- Learn new things about yourself.
- Spend time talking to a lonely neighbor.

SAGITTARIUS

Sagittarius is the seeker of truth through travel, talking to others, and study. As the adventurers of the Zodiac, people born in Sagittarius use knowledge to fuel their broad-minded approach to life. Keenly interested in philosophy and religion as aids to their inner quest, they typically are clear thinkers with a love of freedom and movement. But they know that a mind is more effective and powerful when there's a strong body to go with it. Many Sagittarians are athletic, possessed of agile bodies and great stamina. They have a desire to explore the far reaches—of the world, of ideas, of their own being.

Sagittarians can be impatient if their thirst for adventure and learning isn't slaked as quickly as they'd like. Zeal thwarted can turn into testiness, self-righteousness, and a tendency to judge harshly. Left unchecked, that hunger for knowledge can become a kind of intellectual gluttony.

Mercury Direct in Sagittarius

Your mode of expression is impulsive, direct, and to the point. You want to get to the bottom line quickly and may upset gentler souls in the process. You often express what's on your mind with a childlike quality, full of wonder and trust. You have little use for politics, preferring to promote your own views and opinions of things. To your surprise, people sometimes see you as intolerant.

Despite such tendencies, your intelligence and desire for knowledge make you an excellent teacher. You pierce the heart of an issue quickly, presenting your ideas to others simply but with a flair for drama. A lifelong student, you strive for truth and possess the courage to question accepted theories. In your quest to find the meaning of life, you are attracted to theology and philosophy. But you can lose your focus if something else comes along to capture your attention. The secret is to keep your goals before you at all times.

MR in Sagittarius

Your mind is sincere and honest but may also be impatient and restless. You are well served by focusing on the here and now instead of going off on tangents or looking into the future. Your wish to understand everything all at once can cause you to get lost in the vastness of it all. You have so much to say that at times you don't know where to begin—and so you don't. During MR many Sagittarians suffer from a kind of chronic writer's block.

Still, there is a visionary quality about you. You can see things others often do not see, and your thinking can take you to uncharted territories. You are a kind of mystical messenger of truth, presenting insights others may miss.

How Sagittarius Survives During
Mercury Retrograde

If Sagittarius is the adventurer, then Mercury Retrograde is a time with great potential for misadventure. Bud is a living testimony to what can happen. A college student in Oregon, Bud was excited by a course he took in Eastern philosophy. He wanted to enrich his knowledge with some firsthand experience. So he booked a tour that would take him to the spiritual capitals of Asia—Kyoto, Tibet, Nepal, and India. Unfortunately, he didn't realize that his three-week odyssey was scheduled smack dab in the middle of M℞.

You can predict the consequences. He caught his flight, but because of bad weather it was rerouted. He had to skip Japan entirely and wound up in Singapore. He made it to China, but because of political turmoil there the border to Tibet was closed. He managed to hook up with a tourist group headed for the Himalayas, but bad weather made it impossible for him even to glimpse Mount Everest. He ended up in New Delhi, broke and hungry, ready to head home—when his luggage, including his return ticket, was stolen. A kindly couple he met at the U.S. Consulate loaned him the money to fly home.

All was not lost, however. Bud wrote an article about his adventure and sold it to a leading travel magazine. He used the money to pay back his benefactors. He's also sworn never to plan a trip when Mercury is headed in the wrong direction. "Before I plan to see any more of Earth," Bud remarked, "I plan to take a closer look at the stars."

Sagittarius Mercury Retrograde Survival Tips

- Curb your urge to travel; instead travel mentally by learning about new countries and different cultures.
- Investigate new courses of study—but don't enroll yet.
- Spend an active but relaxing day at the beach or at the spa.
- Call an elderly relative and lift his spirits.

CAPRICORN

Although their symbol is the goat, Capricorns tend to be anything but frivolous and capricious. The pragmatists of the Zodiac, they often adopt a no-nonsense, prudent, businesslike approach. To a Capricorn, life can be one big project (or lots of little projects, one after the other). Ambitious and determined, they work hard to succeed. They usually reach the top, if that's their goal, but they do so at a slower pace than their competitors. Industrious, efficient, patient, and disciplined, they know the value of taking one step at a time. More like tortoises than hares, they know that "slow and steady" is likely to win them the race.

At the other extreme, someone born in Capricorn can be maddeningly inhibited, even rigid. You often feel you have to drag them into anything—making a decision, going to a social event, taking that next big commitment. Once they make up their minds, they move ahead with gusto—but they'll still usually take it just one step at a time. At worst, a Capricorn can seem melancholy and fearful, believing that disaster is just around the corner.

Mercury Direct in Capricorn

Your thinking is clear and methodical, but you can be rigid. You are more at home in the material world than in the abstract world of ideas. As a result, you can be very successful in business. You can set your goals and work toward them with quiet persistence and determination.

After reaching one goal, you won't spend a lot of time exulting. Instead, you'll set the next target and take the first step toward reaching it.

You have good powers of concentration, but typically these skills don't emerge until later in life. You may have left school earlier than most—but if so, you will be all the more determined to catch up later. You have a special need to prove yourself. Once you've made up your mind to do so, you apply yourself to your education. You may not be ready for college at the traditional time in life, but once enrolled you will do very well.

Unlike Sagittarius, your astrological neighbor, you are not naturally spontaneous. You tend to weigh your words before you speak. You do not form ideas lightly, nor share them without due consideration. Because of this, others seek and value your opinions on a range of issues.

MR in Capricorn

You are a deep and serious thinker. As a child, you may do things the hard way and make mistakes. Still, you can learn from your mistakes more readily than most. You can reconstruct what went wrong and you have the discipline to ensure that you do not make the same mistakes again. When young, you may have gone through periods of depression and pessimism as you struggled to understand what life is about. As you got older, though, you discovered that your methodical ways built a firm foundation for your choices, contributing to your success and showing you how to make the most of the resources at your disposal.

You enjoy social events, especially those with a serious purpose, such as readings or lectures. You love to take part in discussions about historical or political topics, especially if you have some special expertise to contribute. You are a person who excels at public speaking. You can discuss serious issues with clarity, dignity, and precision.

How Capricorn Survives During Mercury Retrograde

Jeremy prides himself on his practical frame of mind. As a civil engineer, he likes working on projects that have useful goals. His greatest achievement, he says, was the redesign of a highway interchange that had been causing traffic tie-ups for years. After Jeremy's work, the bottlenecks disappeared and traffic flowed smoothly. He's a loving father and uncle, and he has earned quite a reputation for the types of gifts he gives. They're always practical: tools, gadgets, gizmos. Once someone gave him a gag gift—a beanie hat with a propeller on top. Jeremy was perplexed. "What am I supposed to do with this?" he asked. A few days later he found his own answer: He used the propeller to make a "personal fan," and used the cloth from the beanie to patch a hole in the seat of his favorite pair of jeans.

But MR can throw Jeremy off his stride. He's found that during these periods it's harder for him to think clearly. He makes lots of little errors in his blueprints and plans—errors that, if not caught, would cause huge, expensive problems during construction.

In keeping with his nature, Jeremy has discovered a practical solution to MR. He doesn't fight it. Instead, he celebrates it. He rents an armful of comedy videos and spends an entire evening laughing himself silly. He visits a toy store and buys the most useless fad items he can find, distributing them to the kids in his neighborhood. He invites friends over for an evening of music using only handmade instruments—kazoos, tissue-paper combs, bongos made of oatmeal boxes. To his delight, he's found that indulging in such moments actually sharpens his thinking and renews his interest in the complex and detailed projects before him.

Capricorn Mercury Retrograde Survival Tips

- Revise your plans thoroughly to ensure the foundations are solid.
- Hike to the top of your nearest hill or mountain, but don't forget the sunscreen, water bottle, and Band-Aids.
- Look around for a better job, but don't leave your current one.
- Give a generous donation to your favorite charity.

AQUARIUS

Aquarians are humanitarian, philanthropic, and keenly interested in making the world a better place. Known as the reformers of the Zodiac, they are progressive souls who love to spend time thinking about how things can be better. They are inventive, original, freedom loving, and individualistic. They seek out the new and different, the innovative, the unique. More than most people, they often keep one eye on the future, always believing that a better day is coming, that a more humane and altruistic world is not only possible but imminent. The Age of Aquarius, indeed!

At the other extreme, Aquarians can sometimes be fanatical and rebellious. Pursuing freedom for freedom's sake, they can become detached from the consequences of their actions, running the risk of being thoughtless, unfocused, perhaps a bit anarchistic.

Mercury Direct in Aquarius

You are one of a kind: original and progressive. Because you're ahead of the flock, others sometimes regard you as eccentric—but you don't mind that. You have a healthy respect for tradition, but not if it is outmoded. You have a lot of respect for people if they earn it, but you definitely do not respect position for its own sake.

As a humanitarian with a strong sense of fair play, you like to espouse causes. Often your causes are considered controversial—even revolutionary. You just like to stay ahead of your time. People are attracted to you for your intuitive mind and understanding of the human soul. Although sociable and adept with words, both spoken and written, you can be aloof. You are not a snob; instead, you can be more like an absentminded professor living in a slightly different dimension. Even so, you can effectively put your ideas into action, once you set your mind to the task, and especially if doing so serves a noble cause.

MR in Aquarius

This is a good position for Mercury Retrograde. Mercury in Aquarius always gives an original mind, but the retrograde position somehow makes it even more unique. At worst you are cranky and eccentric, but at best you are something of a genius in the mental world. You have such a wide range of ideas that, although people may not always feel you have your feet on the ground, they cannot deny your originality.

You are sometimes ahead of your time. You have the ability to look forward into the future and have an innate feeling for global, revolutionary ideas that will benefit the whole of humankind. You will be among the first people to see the value in gadgets and equipment that are new and useful, such as a solar-powered house or car. You often can see the value in things that other people may miss. This is because you are yourself an inventor at heart. You are especially good at drawing upon old ideas and updating them for the good of humanity.

How Aquarius Survives During
Mercury Retrograde

In college Greg was, as he puts it, "quite a rabble rouser." If there was a student protest, he was there, in the front of the line. "I organized a boycott of nonunion lettuce, I marched in civil rights marches, I picketed unfair labor practices." Articulate and driven, Greg was a media darling. Interviewers picked him for their feature stories because they knew they'd always get a good quote out of him. A typical comment: "I'm doing this for the kids—my kids, your kids, and kids yet to be born. They deserve a better world. We all do." Since his college days, Greg has held a number of responsible positions in nonprofit organizations, doing good works here and abroad.

But he knows that Mercury Retrograde can wreak havoc on his life. During one such period, he recalls, he had organized a protest march for animal rights. But the flyers he printed up had the wrong location. "I was the only one there," he remembers. "Everyone else was waiting for me across town." A newspaper reporter once misquoted him, and he was hit with a massive lawsuit for libel. He collected thousands of dollars in contributions for a group that does medical work in poor countries, but discovered to his shock that a computer hacker had broken into his bank's computer and drained the account.

Like a good Aquarian, Greg has figured out strategies to cope with M℞. When possible, he avoids scheduling large-scale events for these weeks. Instead, he devotes his energies to reviewing past events and incorporating the lessons learned into his future programs. He tries not to book travel during these times, and if he must go somewhere he allows lots of breathing room in the schedule for delays or canceled flights. He also refuses to give interviews or to write anything for publication. "Actually, I find Mercury Retrograde to be a blessing in disguise," he says. "It's a chance to take a step back, recharge my batteries, and find renewed energy to tackle the issues that matter most to me."

Aquarius Mercury Retrograde Survival Tips

* Plan the rally you had envisioned to help the homeless, but don't schedule it just yet.
* Resist your urge to join another a new group or voluntary organization until you have investigated its aims and objectives thoroughly.
* Don't break a friend's confidence—it could backfire.
* Study astrology.

PISCES

People born under Pisces tend to be selfless, spiritual, and focused on feelings. They are often visionaries, imbued with a sense of wonder about the world and its mysteries. Known as the illusionists of the Zodiac, they may have a special knack for creative expression, especially in the arts but also in music. The intuition of the Pisces-born is highly evolved. They are compassionate, kind, charitable, and self-sacrificing.

At the other extreme, Pisces people may feel a strong need to escape from reality. If their sensitivity is too highly developed, they may fall prey to a kind of helplessness. Overly trusting, they may not see the danger lurking behind an attractive image or a pleasant feeling. As a result, they may be more prone to addictive or codependent behaviors than those born under other signs.

Mercury Direct in Pisces

Your mind is receptive, impressionable, and ruled by your feelings. Because of this, you have a rich fantasy life, which may lead you to find the mundane world rather harsh. You enjoy art, beauty, music, and all the things that make you feel good. Your sensitivity to the unseen world gives you an almost psychic ability to know what other people are feeling. Consequently, you follow your gut instincts rather than reason. At the same time, this ability can make you too sensitive; you can become moody and withdrawn.

You are a natural recluse who inclines toward spiritual pursuits such as prayer and meditation. You see the good in everyone—or at least want to. Such a quality will bring you true friendships, but it can also expose you to people who will drain you. You are well advised to consult your mind, as well as your gut feelings, when judging the value of something.

MR in Pisces

Trying to separate your conscious mind from your intuition can lead to confusion. You sometimes feel as if you are in a fog. Instead, consider taking up hobbies and activities that do not involve your conscious mind—gardening, painting, or music. Such things will reward you by bringing you greater clarity to your feelings.

You may lack confidence in your mental abilities, since other people do not always understand what you are trying to communicate. Bear in mind (and in heart) that your understanding is so deep that it may be hard for you to explain yourself using mere words. For example, if you are with someone who is lonely or depressed, you can feel the pain as if it were your own. It is as if you have a psychic antenna to things that lie beneath the surface of life, such as feelings and vibrations. It is often difficult for you to verbalize what you feel, however, and express it clearly to others. Your sensitivity gives you the capacity for great compassion. It will be beneficial if you channel this through caring for others.

How Pisces Survives During Mercury Retrograde

Marianne is a nurse who often takes on the toughest assignments. She's worked in the burn unit, in the psychiatric ward, in the neonatal intensive care department. Her most recent work has been in a hospice, treating people who are dying from cancer. Her friends and family wonder how she can take the strain of being around so much pain and suffering. "I try to remember it's their pain, not mine," she says. "I use my strengths to help them through this passage."

She's learned that there are times when the pressure can get to her. Many of those times coincide with MR. The nature of her work makes it virtually impossible for her to just step away for a few weeks. Too many people depend on her skills.

Instead, she makes sure she schedules enough time to be alone in quiet reflection. She's found a spot on the grounds of a nearby college where she can go and sit for a while, savoring the view and practicing some gentle breathing exercises. During MR she pays particular attention to the foods she eats, choosing things she doesn't normally have and experimenting with unusual cuisines. She also makes a point of sketching or painting for half an hour or so each day—abstract shapes and images, unencumbered with conscious intent. At the end of the retrograde, she glances over her sketches. If she discovers something of value, she'll often paste the image onto a handmade card and deliver it anonymously to one of her patients. Otherwise she's as likely to burn her sketchbook in a small, private ceremony of personal release. As the paper is consumed by the fire, Marianne says, she feels a sense of rededication to her purpose.

Pisces Mercury Retrograde Survival Tips

- Channel your desire for emotional excess through prayer and meditation.
- Recharge your batteries by spending time in nature; commune with the trees and plants.
- Paint, listen to music, and tend your garden.
- Volunteer at your local hospital.

The MR℞ Effect and the Houses

Every aspect of human experience falls into categories: work, home, money, career, relationships, and so on. In astrology the twelve Houses (see table 5) represent those realms of experience common to all of us.

The planets move through each of the Houses of your birth chart at some point during the course of their celestial wanderings. As they do, they each exert their unique influence.

For example, when Mercury travels in the Sixth House, work and health, communication on the job or with your doctors may become particularly important. Mercury Direct may indicate that you should make a special effort to keep the lines of communication open—returning phone calls, responding to memos, making it to that doctor's appointment on time. Mercury Retrograde, in contrast, suggests you should be on guard against communication breakdowns in the office or with respect to medical matters.

To see where Mercury is headed today, check the ephemeris in appendix 1. If you want to get the most accurate assessment of Mercury's effects on the Houses in your own life, however, you'll need to have a copy of your birth chart handy. If you do not already have a chart, see Resources in the back of the book to learn how to obtain a free copy of your birth chart.

TABLE 5:
The Birth Chart Showing Signs and Houses

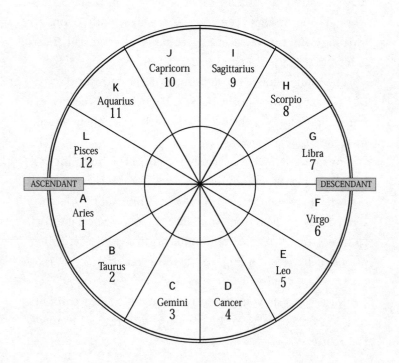

GUIDELINES TO FIND OUT HOW MERCURY AFFECTS YOU TODAY

Here's how the process works.

1. Check the ephemeris in appendix 1 to find out in which sign Mercury is today, and also whether it is direct or retrograde. (Remember, if today's date is not listed, go to the nearest date before it.)
2. If, for example, you see Mercury is in the sign of Pisces today (the symbol is ᴸ), you then look at where the sign of Pisces is in your own birth chart. This will indicate which part of your birth chart is highlighted by Mercury—and therefore how Mercury is affecting you today.

   Note: Because the twelve signs of the Zodiac move round your birth chart constantly, Pisces may have been in any of the twelve Houses when you were born. Every birth chart is different.
3. If you see that the Pisces symbol (ᴸ) appears at the beginning (the cusp) of your Seventh House, you will know that **MR** is exerting influence over Seventh House matters, which include your relationships with other people.
4. Because Pisces rules nonverbal communication, the imagination, and daydreaming, a simple interpretation for having Mercury Retrograde traveling through your Seventh House could be: Awkwardness and evasiveness (Pisces) in your communication (Mercury) with other people (Seventh House).

5. By now you know that a retrograde period is not a good time for you to try to explain a complex issue involving a lot of detail (like writing this chapter!). Once you know Mercury Retrograde is in your Seventh House of relationships, you might consider writing down your instructions, or using some other form of communication. Here's a hint: A picture is worth a thousand words.

Another example might be as follows. You look up where Mercury is today in the ephemeris. You see it is direct in Aries. Then you look at your birth chart and see that Aries is on the cusp of your Tenth House. Tenth House matters include career, vocation, and your social standing. Aries is direct and forthright and represents the warrior. You would see from this that (if other parts of your birth chart support it) this could be an excellent day to ask your boss for a promotion!

Note: When traveling directly, Mercury remains in each House and sign for about two to three weeks. When it is retrograde, it can remain in a particular House in your birth chart for more than two months.

THE MEANING OF THE HOUSES

Please note that what follows is only a rough guide to this subject. Everyone's birth chart is different, and is filled with lots of intersecting influences. The Houses are associated with a long list of qualities and associations, some of which are covered in chapter 2. It's not possible to cover all of them in a short chapter. Also, timing is everything; depending on the exact time of day, some portion of a Sun sign might actually be falling into the previous House. Consider consulting an astrologer for help in working out some of these details. But over time, as you explore the concept of Mercury Retrograde, you'll become more sensitive to its influences in different parts of your life. As a consequence, you'll be self-aware, more skilled in adapting to the influence of the planets, and more adept at receiving their important gifts.

THE FIRST HOUSE (ASCENDANT)— THE HOUSE OF SELF

The First House is the segment of your birth chart that begins in the nine o'clock position and heads south to eight o'clock. The beginning of the First House is commonly known as your Ascendant or Rising Sign. This is the sign that was rising on the eastern horizon at the moment you were born. In astrological terms, it's the sign that serves as a metaphoric mirror through which you look and through which others see you. It is your outward image, which reflects your inner being. Thus the First House is known as the House of self. When planets travel across your Ascendant into your First House, you feel an urge to define who you really are—both for yourself and for others in your life. This House—at the beginning of your chart—also represents new beginnings. When planets highlight your First House, it is time to find out who you really are, express yourself, and enjoy life. Through the conscious choices you make through your First House, you can move from selfishness toward true self-confidence.

Mercury Direct in the First House

Here's a personal example to show how you might respond to the appearance of Mercury in your First House. Not long ago I checked my horoscope and learned that, indeed, Mercury was traveling over my Ascendant. Given my understanding of the significance of that event, I knew it was an opportune time to improve some aspects of myself and my life that I suspected needed some attention.

On the physical level I tidied up some of the clutter around me. I sorted through my closet—a task long overdue—and collected bags of clothes to give to Goodwill. Feeling the need to update my appearance, I bought a few new outfits. I relished my new image!

In the mental realm I gave considerable thought to the way I wanted to present myself to the public. With the insights gained, I designed and wrote my personal Web site.

Spiritually speaking, I took a close look at a particular weakness of mine that I had been wrestling with for most of my life; a problem that still nettled me. I spent the time working on this through a combination of reflection, self-analysis, and prayer. Also, given that the teaching of Mercury at this time is to communicate with the world about your sense of self, I prepared a lecture on the subject "Man—Know Thyself" and the importance of examining your own weaknesses in order to overcome them. All this emphasis, in the detached, objective style of Mercury, brought home to me more than ever before that it was time to let go of any prejudices and problems from the past, to renew my sense of living in the present, and to create new opportunities for the future.

Like all the forces we explore in astrology, though, there's a downside. Too much emphasis on self can throw your life out of balance. When exploring your First House, then, I recommend you look at all the levels of your being—your outward appearance as well as your deeper, more spiritual core. The choices you make can determine whether your course is one of personal growth—or self-limitation.

So when you discover that Mercury is transiting your First House, remember that this House represents new beginnings. Make positive choices about yourself and your future. Have fun; be self-contained and self-possessed, but not selfish.

MR in the First House

If you find that Mercury is in retrograde in your First House, seize this opportunity to learn about your deepest desires. Curb your impulsive tendencies to do new things and communicate with others, and spend more time by yourself. Don't make blunt comments to others without first thinking about the effect of your remarks. Be sensitive. During the day, take note of things you said or did that had a direct impact on your situation. Make an honest appraisal: Did these things help or hinder you as you pursued your goals? If you find that you didn't do yourself any favors, first forgive yourself. Then make a pact with yourself to do better the next day.

One of my clients, Zoe, told me a story that drives home the point. She had decided to apply to graduate school and earn a degree in computers. She'd worked in technology for years, but felt she couldn't go anywhere without more education.

She consulted her chart and discovered that Mercury was in retrograde, but application deadlines were looming and she went ahead and sent out her forms. To her dismay, two of the three applications went astray in the mail. The third school accepted her—but didn't give her the financial aid she needed.

Feeling miserable, Zoe went to a local coffee shop where she drowned her sorrows in cappuccino. She started chatting with the elderly woman sitting next her and told her the sad tale. The woman commented, "Everything happens for a purpose." Then she added, with a twinkle in her eye: "Obviously, my dear, you are barking up the wrong tree."

Somehow, those words hit Zoe with all the force of timeless truth. She suddenly realized that she didn't really want to go to school—what she wanted was the courage to start her own business. Her years of experience had taught her enough to get going. Today she runs a computer consulting business. Although she's working harder than ever, she's happy and making lots of money. Zoe's time during Mercury Retrograde would have been better spent thinking about what she really wanted to do with her life rather than sending out applications to schools she didn't really want to attend—and that were bound to go astray.

THE SECOND HOUSE—
VALUES AND POSSESSIONS

This is the House concerned primarily with the role of money in your life, and by extension the possessions money can buy. In a larger sense, though, the term *values* also refers to intangibles—including talents and qualities—that you believe are important, or that you hold on to for security. In this House are found your entire set of resources: physical, mental, and spiritual.

Mercury Direct in the Second House

The influence of Mercury in this House probably will have to do with the way your money moves through your hands. You might have to communicate with your banker or stockbroker, and this would certainly be an excellent time to study your financial portfolio. Depending upon other factors in your birth chart, it may also be a good time to invest money in the stock market, real estate, or art.

Because the Second House also represents things of the senses—art, music, food, wine, and so on—you may find yourself visiting the theater more than usual or dining out more frequently. Another reason to be thinking about your finances!

On a deeper level, when Mercury transits your Second House, it is a good time to think about the people and ideals you value, and why you value them.

MR. in the Second House

You'd be wise to examine your bank statements and records carefully to make sure all is in order. This isn't the best time to undertake financial transactions. A couple of years ago, during Mercury Retrograde, I transferred a large sum of money from my bank in Los Angeles to family members in London. Although my bank did not hesitate in removing funds from my account, the bank in England did not receive the money. After dozens of phone calls over several weeks, the money was finally found and the transaction was finally complete. I then found that my bank had charged me a fat fee for all the work they had done! It took another few phone calls to get this reimbursed. Yes, I know I should have known better . . .

Check your stock listings—it's possible some of your holdings may plummet during a retrograde period (especially communications and telco stocks!). If so, just hold tight. This is not the time to panic and make impulsive decisions about your finances. This is a good time to take a complete inventory of your resources and see if there are ways they can be made to work better for you.

Also, give yourself the time and space you need to get your priorities straight. Ask yourself: What are the most important things in my life right now?

Here's how Madge handled these circumstances. For as long as I'd known her, I'd listened to her complain about her husband. Jerrod, some years older than she was, had become quite ill and was no longer able to work much. Madge is a kind and compassionate soul who devotes much of her time to charity—running fund-raising efforts, driving the elderly on errands, and so on. But with an ailing husband at home, she was no longer able to be as involved in her causes as she would have liked.

During a recent **MR** Jerrod suffered a heart attack and had to be rushed to the hospital. While he recovered, Madge had time alone in the house. She realized how much she missed him and how much she loved him. She admitted that she had begun to think of him as a burden. But now she saw how much of an emotional anchor he was for her. He was always willing to listen to her stories, to offer insights and perspective, and—this was especially important to her—to laugh at her jokes and wisecracks. She came to see that his illness was a blessing in at least one respect, because he was more available to her. And he always made a point of thanking her for the effort she spent tending to his needs.

Madge decided to reevaluate her priorities and began devoting herself more thoughtfully to his care. He recovered beautifully and was able to go back to work nearly full time. This in turn led to more financial stability. Madge and Jerrod found themselves happier than they'd been for years. As she told me later, she was grateful that her encounter with **MR** taught her to value others, especially her husband.

THE THIRD HOUSE—COMMUNICATION

This House represents your powers of communication and your ability to learn through the application of your conscious mind using logic, reason, and curiosity.

(Learning through intuition or inspiration is represented by the Ninth House.) The Third House reflects your ability to deal with different types of people. Also involved in this House are brothers, sisters, and neighbors, your willpower, and transportation.

Mercury Direct in the Third House

When Mercury transits your Third House, you will probably find yourself busy handling lots of tasks involving everyday communication—telephone calls, errands, e-mails. You might find yourself on the go more than usual, especially for short local trips. This is a good time to improve your communication skills, especially with your siblings or neighbors. This would be a great time to plan a family reunion or invite the neighbors over for dinner.

Your mind will likely be more open and responsive to ideas. You might even discover that you become more adept at carrying on amusing conversations during these times. Less tolerant of boring routine, you'll feel hungry for freedom and unusual ways of expression. Allow yourself the opportunity to benefit from this time: Go out, take advantage of social invitations, be joyful, expressive, and creative. Try something new.

MR in the Third House

When Mercury runs retro, it may be an opportune moment to review your relationships, especially with your brothers, sisters, and neighbors. Don't say things to them you might regret later. Take a look at your life and see if you feel you are meeting your need for creativity and fresh insights. It's a good time for study, but don't enroll for any classes just yet. You may regret your choices later.

A man named Alex had been working on his novel for more than a year and was feeling stuck. During our consultation he learned that Mercury was retrograde in his Third House. We talked about the potential impact of that phenomenon for a while. Suddenly his eyes lit up. "I think I've got it!" he said. That night he went home and tried writing in a completely new way. He created the last line of a story, then wrote the paragraph before it, then one before that. He ended up with a tale unlike anything he'd created before. I asked if it was any good. "Nope!" he said laughing. "It stinks!" But it was still one of the best things he'd ever written, he continued, because it freed his mind to work in a new and productive way. His creative logjam cleared, he returned to work on his novel with renewed vigor. A year later I was delighted to see his book on display at our local store.

THE FOURTH HOUSE—ROOTS AND HOME

This is the House of the home, the inner self. It is where you put down roots and lay foundations. The home environment nurtures you so that you feel comfortable and secure. The Fourth House also represents the ultimate security figure, Mother, as well as family history and heritage. Here is where you'll find endings—the end of a problem, of a trend, of life.

Mercury Direct in the Fourth House

When Mercury transits your Fourth House, you may yearn for privacy and peace and feel a desire to develop your inner life by examining yourself honestly. Perhaps you'll feel drawn to books (like this one) that offer ideas about exploring aspects of your being and improving your daily life. You will certainly feel more sensitive than usual, and this is a good time to nurture yourself: Light some candles, pick up a good book, and take a long, hot, luxurious bath.

Importantly, you may feel a need to put things you've studied into practice. No longer satisfied with ideas, you want to see action! This is an ideal time to study interior design or Feng Shui. Also, if you are thinking of buying or selling a home, this may be a good time to do so.

Unwilling to be a follower, you will find the courage to think differently, to find your own path and discover your own truth. You might discover an urge to search for a reality that can unite rather than divide.

MR in the Fourth House

This is a good time to reflect on your childhood, to revisit the routines you've held on to over the years and see if they still serve your deeper interests. I often urge people to rethink their personal goals during these moments, to look at them from a broader perspective. Consider reevaluating relationships with those close to you, particularly your mother. Look for opportunities to bring closure to unresolved issues, especially those that have been lingering since childhood or that you have long desired to move past. You may feel an urge to redecorate or renovate your home or move into a new one. Remember—what looks good now may not look so good later when Mercury goes direct. Investigate real estate agents if you must, but don't buy your dream home just yet.

Frieda told me that her father had abandoned the family when she was still a baby. She had seen him occasionally, but it had been years since they'd last spent time together. Despite her parents' divorce, she felt he was a special person, a good man. But for as long as she could remember, Frieda's mother, embittered, had derided him, criticizing everything about him. Her comments were a constant source of friction between them. Frieda felt compelled to defend him against her attacks. Gradually she started to withdraw, not wanting to spend time at her mother's because she knew that the topic of her father would dominate their time together.

But during MR in the Fourth House, Frieda came to a realization: It didn't matter that she saw things differently from her mother. They could agree to disagree. Importantly, she realized that she was capable of loving both of her parents. Some weeks later (when Mercury was direct!) she expressed this to her mother and found that the barrier between them dissolved. What's more, her mother at last acknowledged that he was indeed a good man, and that she was equally to blame for their separation. Frieda's realizations had brought renewal to them both.

THE FIFTH HOUSE—
PLEASURE AND CREATIVITY

The Fifth House represents the creative, playful side of you. Creativity is in fact an act of giving. When you create, you give something of yourself and convert it to something else—a painting, a song, a poem, or a delicious meal. This House also indicates the child within you and indicates how you relate to children, pleasure, and simple fun. It shows how you find emotional satisfaction and represents your willingness to take risks with love and money. The Fifth House is associated with gambling—and it isn't hard to see a connection between these two concepts! Both offer ways that people seek pleasure and emotional excitement through taking chances. Life is more than just being or doing. Life also means seeking pleasure in the things you do.

Mercury Direct in the Fifth House

When Mercury transits this House, you feel impelled to seek creative outlets and new forms of expression. This would be a great time to write, play the piano, paint, or just take the kids out and enjoy life! You may find yourself wanting to plan a party for no particular reason—go ahead and do so. If you do not have children, you may find yourself browsing through baby books in the local bookstore—children may definitely be on your mind. It can be a lucky time, so don't forget to buy your lottery tickets. I don't guarantee a win, but you'll enjoy the gamble.

MR in the Fifth House

With Mercury Retrograde, you may find yourself questioning why you love what you do. An old flame may suddenly reappear in your life, if only in your thoughts. That person's appearance might present a challenge, calling on you to examine past relationships and discover what you learned. You may feel dissatisfied with a current love interest—but don't make any rash decisions now.

Use this opportunity to review your outlets for self-expression and creativity. Are you satisfied with these outlets? Have you become stale and stuck in routines? Might there be new ways you can find that reveal the facets of your personality whose sparkle has been lost over the years?

A client, Robert, told me that he was poking around on the Internet one day (I probably don't need to mention that it was when Mercury was retrograde in his Fifth House). On a whim, he decided to type in the name of an old girlfriend he hadn't seen in more than a decade. Sure enough, he found Marsha's Web site—she ran an online resource for people interested in gardening. Seeing her picture and reading her name triggered a flood of memories and associations. Robert has been happily married for eight years. "But I have to admit," he said, "for about a week I found myself obsessed with thinking about her—wondering how she was doing, how she felt about her life, whether she ever thought about me."

For some marriages, this might have been a disaster. But both Robert and his wife, who had been consulting their horoscopes together since they'd met, realized that an opportunity lay before them. They explored the nature of their relationships and what they'd gleaned from each one. Robert felt that knowing Marsha had taught him how to be more willing to give the other person emotional and spiritual room to express creativity. His wife had benefited from that discovery. That's because Robert had made a special effort to help her set up a darkroom where she could print her black-and-white photographs. Rather than being jealous of Marsha—a woman who, for Robert, existed only in the past—she found herself grateful for what that relationship had taught her man.

THE SIXTH HOUSE—
WORK AND HEALTH

Why, you may wonder, does the same House represent such disparate concepts? Is there really a connection between work and health?

Indeed there is. Many people tend to devote too much of their energy to their work at the expense of their other needs. The result: stress, strain, and exhaustion. Consequently, this House is also associated with the need to maintain health, specifically through careful attention to diet, physical exercise, and daily routines. Routines enable you to practice good health while spending a minimum of energy doing so.

This House is also associated with service to others. Spiritually aware people know that the key to health and happiness lies in giving back something of what they have gained in life. Lastly, this House represents your sense of duty, responsibility, and personal growth. Fully realized individuals are those who know the value of serving their own needs and requirements, as well as those of others.

Mercury Direct in the Sixth House

This is a great time to study all aspects of health and healing. A friend of mine took her final examinations in acupuncture when Mercury was traveling through her Sixth House—she passed! I try to schedule my routine health examinations during this time, as it's a good time to think about body maintenance. It's also great for detailed work, such as editing or analysis of some kind. Good for administration, filing, keeping up your calendar and diary, and all those routine tasks that make your world go around more smoothly. You may be thinking about changing jobs; well, now's the time to study the job market and send out your applications. And it's a good time to take on volunteer work as a way of reaching beyond yourself to serve the needs of others.

MR in the Sixth House

This is a good time to reflect on ways you might find to improve your health. Fittingly, in this time when Mercury runs in reverse, an old injury or condition from the past may return. This isn't necessarily something to fear, but take extra care with your workouts. If something happens, it may simply be an opportunity to address an old wound and seek its ultimate healing.

Because the Sixth House also is related to your employment or work, this is not a good time to unload your problems and complaints to your boss or coworkers: However good your motives are, they could backfire. There's never a good time to gossip, but it's particularly harmful now.

It is important now to return all your telephone calls on time and keep records of faxes and e-mails you have sent. Also, you should double-check your appointments.

Now, too, may be a wonderful time to review the ways you work, especially your everyday routines. For some people, MR is a chance to shatter old habits that are no longer of value.

Review your short-term career goals and see whether they are still compatible with your long-term ambitions. Consider talking with colleagues at work to see if they have any insights to share.

I know one woman, Elaine, who worked in an accounting department. Her job didn't involve physical labor, but during audits or at tax time her back frequently gave out. She was often in tremendous pain and was sometimes laid up for days.

During MR in her Sixth House we talked about the connection between these events. She realized that she had come to loathe the routine of her job—not just the daily grind, but the annual cycles. The very predictability of things caused her to tense up long before the time had actually arrived to undertake the tasks. I commented that it was as if she was bracing for a car crash before she'd even turned on the ignition. I could see the light dawn in her eyes. A few weeks later she called to let me know she had quit her job and had taken a position teaching accounting at a business college. She still loved crunching numbers, but now she was able to practice her skill in a new setting and to the benefit of her students. "How's your back?" I asked. "Never better!" Elaine said.

THE SEVENTH HOUSE—
PARTNERSHIPS AND RELATING

The First House is about you; the Seventh House is about how you deal with others. The way you communicate with everyone on a daily basis—doctors, hairdressers, clerks, family, your mate, yourself—is reflected in this House.

This also is the House of partners and partnership. Partners come in many forms—a spouse, a business colleague, a co-captain of the softball team. You communicate differently with each one. Communication can lead to cooperation—or conflict. That's why this House also represents our dealings with the public and, perhaps inevitably, with our enemies.

Mercury Direct in the Seventh House

You may find yourself more chatty than usual. You can communicate well with people in a one-on-one situation and more easily sort out problems and explain things clearly and simply. You may find yourself thinking about loved ones, as well as coworkers and partners: Feel free to express your thoughts and feelings. It's beneficial now to give cards or tokens of your friendship and appreciation so that people know how much you care. It is also an ideal time to receive or give training; depending upon other factors in your chart, this would be a good time to enter into contracts with others, too.

MR in the Seventh House

Here is an opportunity to step back and look at your relationships with partners. Retreat is not surrender; it's a learning opportunity. If your marriage could stand improving, if you're in conflict with others at work, perhaps you'll get the perspective you need to discover a solution.

MR is also a chance to see whether there are partnerships missing in your life. To realize your dreams, you might need to find an ally, someone who has the skills and resources you lack. Or you might feel the time has come to marry. Reaching out to others socially or emotionally is a great gift, one that allows us to grow. Learning to handle conflict expands our understanding and deepens our compassion.

Recently, during MR, I reevaluated my relationship with my medical doctor. I've always considered my doctors as partners. But for years I've been learning all I can about the healing arts and alternative methods. The more I learned, the more I found I was arguing with my physician over his practice of orthodox Western medicine. I believed that, as a healer-in-training myself, I should take more responsibility for my own health and make my own choices about prevention. He was just as adamant that there were some things only he could do to help me stay healthy. At one point he blurted, "You're just as prejudiced against my medicine as I am against yours!" His sudden admission caught us both by surprise, and we laughed.

In the days that followed I mulled over that moment. I realized he was right—that I had allowed my prejudices to cloud my judgment. I thought about the many people whose lives have been saved by brilliant and caring physicians. My attitude shifted, and I felt a greater acceptance for their wisdom and skill. I rediscovered my sense of partnership with my medical caregivers.

Later, when MR had ended, a wonderful moment happened. I was teaching a class about hands-on healing. I discovered to my delight that one of the students was a doctor. He said he was eager to learn any technique that relieved suffering. In my view, the lesson of MR is that, when I surrender part of my prejudice, someone else might do the same.

THE EIGHTH HOUSE—SHARED RESOURCES AND TRANSFORMATION

This House represents the deeper levels of relationships, especially marriage, sex, and power. It contains our experiences regarding our material values. And it includes the realm of death, rebirth, and the ability to transform our lives. At their core, all of these aspects of life are rooted in our deep need for security.

Marriage, for example, is a way of securing companionship on all levels. Sex is our way of regenerating ourselves, to feel secure that we'll survive into the future. Power is a strategy for protecting ourselves, for making sure our will—and not the will of our enemies—is done. Material goods are the most tangible form of security. Many of us surround ourselves with things, as if trying to build a wall of objects that will protect us from the dangers of the world. This House also governs shared resources, such as taxes, insurance, and inheritance.

And death . . . we so greatly fear death that we'll do just about anything to convince ourselves that it will never happen to us. Our experiences to achieve security in the face of inevitable death are represented by the Eighth House.

Mercury Direct in the Eighth House

This is a good time to work on your taxes, as well as streamline insurances and joint financial arrangements. If you are single, marriage may be on your mind. If you are married, this is a great time to talk to your partner about important issues in your relationship. Through honest communication, your marriage can improve and transform into something better. This would be a good time to visit your financial adviser or accountant. It would also be a good time to draw up your will. You might find yourself thinking or reading about subjects such as life after death or reincarnation at this time.

MR in the Eighth House

When Mercury slides back in its path through this House, we have a wonderful opportunity to reconsider what it takes to make us feel secure. Is it lots of money? Is it worldly goods? I know several people who have redis-covered the importance of spiritual exploration during these periods. They realize that the greatest form of secu-rity is a deep-rooted calmness, a sense of connection to the world.

Although you may be dissatisfied with aspects of your marriage and joint financial arrangements, this is not the ideal time to discuss these matters. A few words out of place could result in argument and disputes. Be careful: Don't overextend yourself, and don't throw your personal power around. You can easily upset other people now.

Laurie told me that she considers **MR** in the Eighth House a time to review many areas of her life. She likes to think about how she would live if she knew this was her last day on Earth. She thinks more deeply about the meaning of life and the way in which she is sharing her tal-ents, resources, love, and wisdom with others. She reflects on the inevitable cycles of nature—of birth, life, and death—that are continually taking place, and on how she can bring transformation into her own life through a more conscious effort to live in harmony with God's laws.

I believe that **MR** in the Eighth House can be particu-larly hard on people in positions of power. They are used to having things their way, ordering people around, imposing their will. When Mercury runs in retrograde, though, their worlds often collapse. Their minions become stubborn and disobedient. The edicts they issue are ignored. Their hold on power seems to slip.

Often, though, the most powerful people are those who realize that their strength lies in the ability to let go. Matt,

a CEO for a software development firm, actually looks forward to MR. He schedules company retreats at these
times, during which they play a game he calls "role retro."
The managers each get a chance to challenge one of Matt's
decisions from the previous few months, stating what they
would have done and telling stories about how the out-
comes would have been different. These are freewheeling,
no-holds-barred sessions—often funny, dramatic, and
revealing. "I learn so much during these retreats," Matt
says. "I not only hear about mistakes I've made as the guy
in charge. I also realize how smart the people I hired are,
and how much they have to offer our company."

Like Matt, you may find yourself reevaluating the way
you use power. Are you seeking ways to control others? Or
are you looking for more personal power, as a way to
strengthen your own gifts in service to others?

MR in the Eighth House offers an opportunity for us
to explore our feelings about death and dying. In my own
experience, focusing my attention on those who have
passed on allows me to become more attuned to them.
Their memories, the things they said and did, their influence on my life now and into the future all become more
clear. In a very real sense, these are messages from the
departed, and they tend to occur with greater force and
regularity during these periods. Perhaps you'll discover that
the same thing happens to you.

THE NINTH HOUSE—
TRAVEL AND PHILOSOPHY

In terms of astrology, *travel* refers to going beyond where you are now in every sense of the term—not just physically but mentally and spiritually as well. The Ninth House represents the desire for meaning, and so is sometimes called the House of higher learning. The message of this House is that life is a voyage of discovery, and that the journey—not the destination—is the goal. In a way, the Ninth House builds on the message of the Eighth House to teach us that we can grow beyond the need for emotional security. By moving on, we explore our higher urge for understanding, for realizing and responding to the universal principles that give meaning to our lives.

The Ninth House represents the way you expand your inner and outer life, and also your higher mind. It represents your search for meaning and truth.

Mercury Direct in the Ninth House

When Mercury transits this House, you may be drawn to subjects such as philosophy, astrology, religion, law, and different cultures. This is a great time for travel—mentally and spiritually, as well as physically. Feel free to enroll in a course of study now. Broaden your horizons, learn a foreign language, study other religions, plan a trip abroad, and book the flight. This is also a good time for sport and exercise, as you feel an urge to stretch yourself beyond your usual physical limits.

MR in the Ninth House

Now is a good time to review your personal view of truth. You may feel that your current outlook on the world has limited you in some ways. Perhaps the influence of Mercury during this period is suggesting that you crave more meaning in your life. This is a good time to study, especially to reread a book that inspired you in the past. You may be surprised at how much more you can learn from an old teacher, given the perspective that time and experience brings to bear.

You've already learned that MR can wreak havoc on travel schedules. If you do travel during this time, make sure you are flexible and can roll with the punches. Don't expect everything to run like clockwork—but do expect the unexpected, and enjoy it. Don't take a vacation abroad at this time if you can avoid it—unless it's to revisit a familiar haunt from the past. It is not a good idea to embark on an adventure or visit unexplored territory, as you may find yourself beset with frustrations and difficulties.

Since this is a time for broadening your mind, give yourself time for quiet reflection. Listen to the communications emanating from within, and discover a new or refreshed outlook on life. Make yourself a vessel ready to receive the flashes of intuition from your higher mind.

Tanya likes to use MR in the Ninth House as an opportunity to take what she calls "inner treks." She sets aside time to look back at the major philosophies and ideas that have shaped her journey through life to this point. "I brew a pot of my favorite tea and assemble a pile of some of my favorite books of wisdom. I grab one at random and open to a page and begin reading." Because Tanya writes notes in the margins, she gets to see how her thought process evolves over time. "Sometimes, reading over my comments, I'm amazed at how dense I can be. But other times I'm reassured that I'm still on the right track." Rediscovering these ideas, she says, is like "getting a letter from old and treasured friends."

Stuart will sometimes schedule a trip to his boyhood hometown during MR in the Ninth House. "I love revisiting the people and places that I knew as a kid," he says. "I'm fascinated to see that some things never change, and some change forever." Stuart adds that these journeys make it clear to him that the biggest changes have occurred within himself. Yet he always finds something about himself that has remained constant across the years. "That sense of constancy is like a railing I hold on to as I pass through this life," he says. "It keeps me steady as I keep moving forward."

THE TENTH HOUSE—
CAREER AND SOCIAL STATUS

This House represents your position in the world—your reputation, ambition, status, and vocation. This is the area in which you are most visible to the world, involving the way others perceive and regard you. The Tenth House reflects your goals and aspirations, achievements and rewards, your roles in society at large. Also contained here are experiences involving your employer, your father, and authoritarian figures in your life.

Strange, but true: The status we enjoy often is tied to the career we pursue. Think about it: Often, the first question asked when we initially meet someone is, "What do you do?" It would be a better world, I believe, if our status reflected our deepest qualities of character. Indeed, in some cultures asking about people's work is considered as rude as asking how much money they make.

Mercury Direct in the Tenth House

When Mercury transits this area of your chart, you may feel the need to examine your career goals, as well as your status and prestige. It is a good time to pursue a new career or take advantage of a career opportunity that comes your way. This is an opportunity to consider the impact you're having on other people and society. Are you using your energies for positive goals? Do others benefit from the fact that you're alive?

Consider, too, your relationship with authority. Do you resent having to bow to the will of others? Don't hesitate to communicate honestly with your boss; now is a good time to ask for a raise or a change in your responsibilities.

Examine whether you exercise your own authority with compassion and intelligence, or are arbitrary and self-serving. Now is a good time to reflect on these parts of your life and work out how you can improve your relationship to a society at large.

MR in the Tenth House

It often happens that an authority figure from the past reemerges in my life during these periods. I might get a call from an old teacher or learn something new about my parents. I'm careful how I approach those in charge. Unfortunately, this is also a time when I'm likely to get a traffic ticket from a cop!

Some years ago I was offered two jobs at the same time. I chose one, but after a few weeks I was miserable, wishing I'd accepted the other. During **MR** in the Tenth House I received a phone call from the boss at the company whose offer I'd initially refused. She said she'd had an inkling that I was unhappy, and asked me to reconsider. She also sweetened the pot by increasing the salary. Of course, I'd already had my second thoughts—and was happy to accept her well-timed offer. I stayed in that job for many happy years.

The lesson hit home: We often make important, life-changing decisions that we come to regret. If we pay attention, though, the universe might give us a chance to retrace our steps. In my case, Mercury had stopped, gone backward a bit, and offered me the gift of a second chance.

THE ELEVENTH HOUSE—
FRIENDS AND IDEALS

This House represents your contacts with other people, both individuals and groups. Especially relevant here are the ways these relationships reflect your ideals and values. Sometimes this is considered the House of hopes, because it involves your sense of idealism, wishes, likes, and dis-likes.

It is within this House that you fulfill personal needs that, ideally, harmonize with the needs of society as a whole. Consequently, this House reflects large groups, especially volunteer organizations, clubs, and professional societies. In this House are the people you choose as friends—and also the kind of friend you are to others. The energy at work here is philanthropy—your ability to put aside selfish, ego-centered desires and devote yourself to others.

Mercury Direct in the Eleventh House

When Mercury travels through this House, you may sense it's time to communicate with your circle of friends, especially someone you'd like to know better. Think about what friendship means to you, and express this to your friends. Be open; you may find that new people are attracted into your life now.

It may also represent an opportunity to volunteer your services to a worthy cause or join a group or organization involved in social reform. We're all busy and pulled in many directions, but sometimes stepping outside our-selves helps us rediscover what's important in life. Now is a good time to do this. It's time to develop our social conscience and realize that we're all part of one family—humankind.

MR in the Eleventh House

During this period old friends from the past may get in touch with you. You may also feel a need to reevaluate your current friendships and make sure they are serving both your interests and the interests of others.

I know several people who, when **MR** is in the Eleventh House, have taken a hard look at certain relationships. They discover that on some levels these "friends" are not friends at all; that they can be selfish or demanding or hurtful. As a result, they decide to invest their time and energy volunteering at hospitals or for community groups. Almost inevitably, they meet new friends and develop other, more satisfying relationships.

Howard told me about his remorse over having "dropped" a longtime buddy. "It got to the point where this guy was draining too much out of me," he said. "He borrowed things and never returned them. He was always a little short of cash, so I'd spot him for a cup of coffee or spring for his movie ticket. He'd pick my brain and then claim my ideas were his own. I didn't mind really—well, maybe a little. But he almost never reciprocated in kind. I stopped returning his phone calls and eventually he got the message. But I feel guilty about it."

As we talked, Howard came to realize that sometimes, by letting go, we gain. Our friends reflect where they are at any one time, intellectually, philosophically, and morally. As we grow, we move on. Our friends do, too. Sometimes letting go allows others to grow in important ways as well. I suggested to Howard that he might think of ending the friendship as a gift, one that would encourage his former buddy to make necessary progress on his own path through life.

THE TWELFTH HOUSE—
BEYOND THE PERSONAL

In this area of your life, you seek peace at the deepest level of your soul. It is here that a gradual growth of awareness is born. Often it takes a deep plunge into suffering and loneliness to discover this awareness. That's why this is also known as the House of self-undoing—but don't be alarmed. What this means is that by drawing on the energy of this House, you undo the ego self, the false self that is built up through years of interaction with others and with society. When you strip away these layers, you rediscover the true self. You come to terms with your core essence, the being that you are and have been and always will be. For that reason, this is also known as the House of reckoning.

As you no doubt realize, the Twelfth House isn't an especially fun place to be. Reflected in this House are such elements as the subconscious mind, secrets, the hidden side of life. Here you may face your most difficult tasks and fight your hardest battles.

On the other hand, the things that cost you the most psychic capital are often the things you come to cherish most profoundly. The aspects of life reflected in this House can be the ones with greatest meaning. This is where your higher self urges you to move forward spiritually (although your lower self may have to be dragged along kicking and screaming). Because of such resistance, you may feel stuck, confined, and lonely.

Mercury Direct in the Twelfth House

This is the time to retreat, contemplate, and meditate on the deeper, spiritual meaning of your life. Turn feelings of loneliness into times when you seek solace and time for yourself. Spend time in the beauty and constancy of nature, by the ocean or high in the mountains. Give thanks for all that you have and all that you are. Feel the presence of a higher power than yourself. Realize that it is here that you stand on the brink of change, looking at everything you have said and done. Here you decide whether to stay where you are, or to allow your consciousness to rise to a higher plane.

MR in the Twelfth House

When **MR** moves through this House, you have an opportunity to achieve closure. You are in a good position to reassess the way you communicate with yourself and with others. You can examine the good and bad qualities of your communication style and prepare to change what needs changing.

Exploring the realm of the inner self is not always a pleasant affair. We may encounter parts of our being that we fear or loathe. Still, many people seem to cling to these negative parts of themselves simply because they are so familiar. The fear of the unknown often prevents us from moving to a new level. But when Mercury runs retro in the Twelfth House, the time has come to confront our subconscious motivations with honesty and openness. Only by doing so will we discover our deepest motivations, our most basic gifts.

For many years Vicky declared herself to be a "devout agnostic." She pointed out that the word *agnostic* means "one without knowledge." She didn't know the answers, but she was determined to find out. She had traveled many paths and explored many avenues, but had never discovered a religious system that addressed her questions or fulfilled her needs.

During a period when M℞ visited her Twelfth House she tripped over a broken stair and sprained her Achilles tendon. Laid up in bed, she was forced to take time off from her job as a personal trainer at a health spa. A visiting friend brought her a book to read: a collection of inspirational essays. She opened the book at random and discovered an excerpt from the first book she had read when she began her spiritual quest more than a decade earlier. The essay contained a description of the nature of God that, in her words, "blew a fuse in my brain." From that moment on, she said, she felt a profound sense of acceptance: She accepted the existence of God, and she realized her own vital part in the divine scheme.

This is a good time to refresh your spiritual life through meditation, prayer, and good works. Make the effort to examine your life and your conscience with all the honesty and simplicity you can. In doing so you prepare yourself for the next cycle, the next turn of the cosmic wheel. Mercury Retrograde offers you this great gift: The chance to move forward in your evolution.

CHAPTER 6

The MR Effect: A Survival Guide

Throughout this book you've read stories of how Mercury Retrograde has affected people and their lives. Hopefully you've also realized that there are lots of strategies you can use to anticipate the impact of the MR effect and to cope with the disasters, large and small, that result.

But I must again emphasize that MR is not necessarily a negative thing. Seen from the right perspective, MR is a kind of gift—an opportunity to discover better, more productive ways of communicating with others, and indeed with yourself. If you consider that MR can be a friend as well as a foe, you can benefit enormously.

In the following pages I'll offer various techniques you can use to take advantage of Mercury's lessons.

RE: **MR** STRATEGIES

It's easy to remember the basic strategy for coping with the
MR effect: Just recall words that start with *re-*. Mercury
Retrograde is a great time to:

- *Review* your life and the decisions you've made.
- *Revisit* the past.
- *Readjust* your priorities.
- *Renew* your capacity to love.
- *Reassure* yourself about your value in this world.
- *Rebuild* shattered relationships.
- *Retreat* to give yourself the space you need.
- *Reclaim* your most important assets.
- *Recommit* to the goals you believe are worthwhile.
- *Reconcile* with people.
- *Recover* from injuries or wounds you've suffered.
- *Redirect* your energies into healthier, more productive
  activities.
- *Redress* past injustices.
- *Reflect* on who you are, where you're going, what you
  have to offer.
- *Recharge* your batteries.
- *Rejuvenate* your spirit through play, laughter, and fun.
- *Repair* any damage you may have caused to objects or
  relationships.
- *Renew* your sense of purpose.
- *Revise* your opinions, attitudes, and routines.
- *Return* to your core set of values.
- *Reward* yourself for success.
- *Remember* that your higher self is in control.
- *Rejoice!*

Resist Using New or Untested Methods of Communication

During MR Erica's answering machine broke down. She's a freelance reporter for several news agencies and absolutely had to have an answering system. The one she bought gave her nothing but grief. It failed to record some messages and deleted others. Often messages were garbled or cut off before they finished. The store gave her a hard time about exchanging the unit. When Erica told me her story, I explained that her unfortunate experience was likely the result of the MR effect. "Why didn't you tell me about this before!" she exclaimed.

During MR electronic gadgets are especially prone to disaster. If possible, resist buying anything involving communications technology during these times. If you must buy something, be sure you have a clear warranty and a liberal exchange policy. Avoid scheduling phone installations, cable TV hookups, and so on. Check the ephemeris and plan to make such moves only after Mercury is again in direct motion.

Refuse to Sign Contracts

Rick, a screenwriter, signed a contract to write scripts for a new TV series. (Need I mention this was during MR?) He's produced dozens of scripts before and is well known in the industry. But this project turned into a disaster. He wrote draft after draft, but the producers rejected each one. Deadlines approached, and Rick went into a panic. Ultimately he was fired for failing to live up to his contract. Making matters worse, the studio sued him for damages. "This project cost me everything," Rick lamented. "My money, my career, and—what's worse—my reputation."

Since the early days of stargazing, astrologers have urged us never to sign contracts during M℞. If ever disaster could befall from a communication breakdown, this is the time. Don't sign up for cell phone service, health club memberships, car leases, or insurance policies. The longer the terms of the contract, the more you should resist! Don't even think about buying a house during M℞.

If you must sign, triple-check everything. Let nothing go unchallenged. If you don't like the terms, change them. (Remember: Everything's negotiable!) If you're not legally inclined, hire someone who is to review the documents. If at all possible, delay putting your name on any document until after Mercury is once again direct.

Respect the Power of M℞

Not long ago I sent out an e-mail to my contact list reminding everyone that M℞ was about to strike and cautioning them to take steps to protect themselves. A few weeks later I received a thank-you gift—a beautiful basket of fruit—with a note from a woman who works as a book designer.

"The day after you sent your warning about M℞, I showed up at my office only to find that my phone lines were out, which meant I couldn't phone, fax, e-mail, or surf the Web. That pretty much brings my business to a halt.

"Then a box I'd been eagerly awaiting arrived—but instead of the photographs I was expecting, it contained about two dozen children's books. They were beautiful, but not what I needed just then for my project.

"Only then did I realize what you'd meant in your warning about **MR**. Although in the past I had let these instances get the better of me, I decided this time I would try some of your suggestions and 'go with the flow.'

"So instead of stressing out over the situation, I turned to tasks that didn't require communication. This was a day to catch up on filing, read up on trends, and take things as they came. I thoroughly enjoyed myself! I knew it was pointless to complain to the phone company (I'd probably wind up on hold anyway), and I told myself the photos I needed would show up eventually.

"Cleaning out files gave me a chance to think through some issues I needed to contemplate, and I came up with some creative solutions to several problems that had been nagging at me. By the end of the day, the phone lines magically cleared up and AOL allowed me access. I even received a call from the person who had sent the books. She realized her mistake just after the shipment went out and invited me to keep them. I decided to donate them to a local charity for underprivileged kids.

"By the end of it, I felt I had beat the system! Instead of spending the day in frustration and confusion, I felt that I had found a way to avoid those little earthquakes that Mercury Retrograde is so famous for.

"What a great day: The closets are cleaned, those children's books are packed and ready to go, and in the end I did manage to communicate with clients—taking care to avoid people for whom I generally have little patience. Of course, I can't sit here and clean closets for the next three weeks until Mercury goes direct again. But I have learned to take MR̥ in stride. I think of this as a good time to 'go inside myself,' make plans for the future, and keep my own peace. I am grateful for my new wisdom and thank you for helping me to bring such order into an otherwise hectic period."

Revise Your Plans

A few years ago my parents bought a car during MR̥—it was a lovely "preowned" BMW. It had just one little problem—the engine tended to cut out at the most inopportune times: in the middle of turns, while sailing down the highway in heavy traffic, or when trying to negotiate a tricky merge. They were lucky they weren't killed. They returned the car to the shop, but it was weeks before the problem was spotted: a faulty weld on a computer chip that controlled the fuel supply.

I urge people never to make a major purchase, especially a car, during MR̥. Even if things seem fine at the time of purchase, there's a good chance a defect will appear during a later retrograde.

Recheck Your Work

Neva, a meeting planner, was in charge of organizing a weekend conference for a major foundation. She gave her okay for print materials being produced by an out-of-town agency. A mailing went out to four thousand prospective attendees, containing all the information they needed—except the date and location of the event. Neva had to print and mail out a corrected flyer, which she had to pay for out of her fees—and that pretty much wiped out her profit. In a delicious irony, the topic of the meeting was "Strategic Communication."

Always double-check your messages during **MR**. Hesitate to press the SEND button on your e-mails until you've read them over. Think: Do I *really* want this to go out over the Net? If possible, ask someone else to read your document to check for typos and other glitches. Don't trust the pharmacy: Triple-check to make sure the prescription is filled properly.

Remember to Keep Your Sense of Humor

Aaron had just moved to L.A. and was eager to set up his bank account. He had a cashier's check representing every penny he owned in the world. The day he filled out the forms was right at the start of **MR**. It took weeks for the check to clear before he could begin drawing out his funds or cashing his paychecks.

Aaron is a laid-back guy with an impish sense of humor. Every day he called the bank to check on the status of his account. Considering the runaround he was being given, he'd have been within his rights to explode in anger. But he kept his cool. Each time he called the woman handling his account, he used a different silly voice and began the conversation with a wisecrack. She'd laugh and check the account—"Nope, no dough yet." Eventually Mercury went direct and the check cleared. And Aaron managed to earn a little unexpected interest: He and the bank clerk are now dating!

RECORD YOUR THOUGHTS

Because Mercury directs communication, it is the governor of our thought processes. The MR effect can cause our thoughts to spin out of control, tumbling out in haphazard fashion. We may feel brain-locked and tongue-tied. MR shatters our routines, disorients us, causes the things we rely on to let us down.

I believe that keeping a journal is a powerful way to regain control over your thought processes. Once you start your MR journal, you will realize there is one thing that never lets you down: your higher self—that spark of divinity within. Keeping track of your ideas helps keep you aware that your higher self is still in charge, always encouraging you, pushing you on toward your dream.

There's no great mystery to the process of keeping a MR journal. Here are some guidelines.

- Buy a special notebook for the occasion.
- During MR periods make it a ritual to write for five minutes at the same time each day.
- Breathe deeply and attune yourself to the deeper part of you. Allow your mind to roam as you gradually take control. Realize that you—your higher self—control your conscious mind; your mind does not control you.

- Start by writing a question. Make your questions broad and expansive ("What can I do to improve my communication with my mate?") rather than petty ("How can I get the money for that new outfit?").
- Listen to the answer as it flows onto your paper. Adopt "stream-of-consciousness" writing; don't censor yourself or worry about spelling and grammar. You are talking to a higher part of yourself, and all you need to do is listen with an open heart.
- Remember the *re-* words. In your journal, recall your day; review events to see how you did; resolve to try new solutions; rededicate yourself to becoming more conscious.
- Do not be led astray. Realize your mind is a tool. Use it wisely, with discrimination, and analyze your answers to see if they are expansive and positive and make sense.
- During your **MR** experiences cultivate attention, curiosity, and wonder. Learn to act and not react to things. Use your journal to record these moments.
- Reinvent yourself and go deeper through your daily ritual of self-examination.
- Find your dreams and follow them; continue to question and to listen.
- Use your **MR** tools of acceptance, faith, love, patience—not anger, frustration, and impatience. You cannot control your environment, only how you choose to act.
- Be open to change and growth after **MR**. Think of these periods as the lull of winter before spring comes.
- Express your new insights and awareness with appropriate right action.

MR MEDITATIONS

In the largest sense, Mercury Retrograde is simply an illusion. In the immediate moment, nothing is moving. There is no going back and no going forward. All there is, is the here and the now. Our task is to make the most of every available moment.

You can catch glimpses of that infinite "now" through the practice of meditation. This ancient art will help you attain detachment and control over yourself. I recommend meditating, especially during MR, because it helps reduce the stress and frustration that arise from thwarted communication. Indeed, meditating is a powerful way to communicate with your higher self.

Following are some meditative exercises you might consider practicing. In the spirit of coping with MR, they are designed to encourage you to reflect on your life, revise it where necessary, renew yourself, and become a more reflective person. I invite you to try practicing one of these a day, perhaps just after you finish writing in your MR journal.

Meditation 1: Refocus

When a student asked his Master how he could gain enlightenment, the Master answered, "Attention." The student asked the Master to elaborate. The Master replied, "Attention, attention, attention!"

Spend today paying attention to what is happening each moment. Keep yourself focused in the present. Watch your mind and wait for the next thought. See how long it takes to come. Now hold that state and pay attention throughout the day, acting appropriately rather than reacting emotionally.

Meditation 2: Recall

Think of the negative things you've said or done over the past few weeks. Then think of the positive things. Analyze which of the two states made you feel good about yourself. Now decide that for today you will only allow positive states of mind, make only positive statements, offer only positive feedback.

Meditation 3: Relax

Close your eyes and lie still. Watch your thoughts as they bubble up; allow them to come and go until your mind becomes still. Now picture yourself walking in a field full of flowers—pink, yellow, blue, moving gently with the breeze. Smell the dampness in the air, feel the warm sun on your face. Ahead of you is a stream. Touch the water, feel it splash over your fingers. Breathe deeply; allow the water to refresh you. Now stand and affirm the beauty and nature around you. Hold this image in your mind's eye for a few minutes. During the day, every hour or whenever you need to, recall this image and allow its peaceful feelings to wash over you.

Meditation 4: Release

Try to release all the thoughts from your mind. Picture your mind as a black slate with nothing written on it. If a thought arises, imagine it is being written on the slate. As soon as the words start to appear, wipe them away until the slate is blank again.

Meditation 5: Rejuvenate

Your breathing is a powerful tool for alleviating stress and anxiety. By slowing down and deepening your breathing, you can also slow down your mind. The result is a powerful feeling of rejuvenation, of calming, centering, and control.

Sit quietly and comfortably and pay attention to your breathing. Inhale slowly and steadily for a count of five, then exhale for the same count. As you inhale, visualize brilliant white light entering you. As you exhale, visualize that all negative energy is leaving you. Continue for at least five minutes. You might want to practice this meditation several times a day.

Meditation 6: Reflect

It's said that when we die, our lives flash before our eyes. We reexperience all the mistakes we've made, as well as all the times we acted with love, courage, and honor. Of course, at that moment it's too late to correct our errors or repeat our noble deeds. But here's an exercise that allows you to do so on a day-to-day basis.

I call this technique "Looking in the Mirror." I practice it regularly and highly recommend it. Sitting quietly and relaxed, recall how you handled your day—the things you said and did, the way you acted. How did these things make you feel? Were you in control? Were you proud of the way you acted? Did you like yourself? As you repeat this "mirroring" process over the course of a few days and weeks, you will start to weed out the things you don't like about yourself. You'll feel those moments coming before they actually strike, and you'll be in a frame of mind that allows you to say, "Oops—that's not a good path to take. I think I'll move in a different direction." As a result, you'll become a more creative, self-controlled, and loving human being.

Meditation 7: Reevaluate

I often found that during times of **MR** I was very impulsive and would spend too much money. Since throughout my life I've struggled with issues of financial security, **MR** could make me monetarily miserable. Once I asked a friend who is both wealthy and generous the secret of his abundance. He said that money is energy, and it likes to flow. If you block the flow of money, you will be broke. But if you allow it to flow, you will have everything you need.

Use this meditation as a way of reviewing your life from the material and financial angle. Simply ponder one or more of these questions and let the answers percolate through your conscious mind: How do I feel about money? Is it something I stash away someplace, thus blocking the flow? Do I buy everything I want, as opposed to everything

I need? Do I ever feel I have enough money? Do I love money or despise it? Am I generous or tight?

If you are not pleased with what you discover about your attitudes toward money, change them. See money as a form of energy that flows through your life like oil to keep things running smoothly. Use your money to make the world a better place. Adopt an attitude of abundance.

Meditation 8: Redefine

Our society rewards hard work, beginning in school, when we struggle to earn good grades. Later we are rewarded with paychecks and promotions. If these goals become ends unto themselves, we risk becoming workaholics. I know; I certainly have many workaholic traits myself.

This meditation addresses issues of work. Once in your meditative mode, contemplate one or more of these questions: Am I defined by what I do or by what I am? Does my work contribute something good to the world, or is it just a way to kill time? Is my work an expression of my deepest sense of self—literally, is it a labor of love? If not, why not? Is it time to redefine what I do?

Meditation 9: Rediscover

Routines have their value: They make it possible for us to move through our day without spending too much energy on choices that don't really matter much in the long run—

what order we perform our morning hygiene rituals; what we have for breakfast; what route we'll take driving to work. By saving our energy, we have more to devote to important tasks. The downside is that routines cause us to become sleepwalkers—we move from moment to moment without thinking, without awareness, without a sense that we're alive. This exercise helps us rediscover what it means to be alive.

Think of an issue that's troubling you: an argument with a lover, a problem with work, concern about money. Now imagine that you aren't the one wrestling with the problem—it's your friend. How would you advise that person? What would you say? Do you have any tools or resources you can offer to help solve the problem?

Meditation 10: Rejoice

Many of the exercises above involve questions about things you might want to change in your life. Now let's take a different tack and celebrate all the things you do *right*.

Get into your meditative stance and contemplate these thoughts: Recall all the good things you said and did and how caring and thoughtful you are. Remember your successes. Reflect on your positive qualities. Make contact with that higher part of you that drives you toward creativity, love, and honor. Respect that part—celebrate it.

MAKE A LIST

Just for fun, here's a list of fifty things to do—and *not* to do—during M℞.

During M℞ you should ...   *But ...*

Return all your phone calls ...	... don't talk too long.
Take a drive in the country ...	... don't forget your map.
Talk nicely to your computer ...	... don't bash it, thump it, or blame it.
Write down information when playing back voice messages ...	... don't rely on your memory.
Reread that contract ...	... don't sign it.
Reread it again ...	... *still* don't sign it.
Smell the roses in your neighbor's garden ...	... don't pick them.
Smile at everyone you meet ...	... don't snap at people who miscommunicate—they're victims of M℞, too.
Compliment your boss's suit ...	... don't tell her what you think of her shoes.
Have a glass of wine before dinner ...	... don't polish off the bottle by yourself.

During MR you should . . .	*But* . . .
Go through your closet and collect donations for charity . . .	. . . don't forget to check the pockets for that missing engagement ring.
Think about getting a new hairstyle . . .	. . . *don't* change hairstyle until Mercury goes direct.
Reflect on past mistakes . . .	. . . don't repeat them.
Tell someone you love him . . .	. . . don't tell someone you hate him.
Tell your mom she's the best parent in the world . . .	. . . don't tell your dad you said that.
Think about buying a new car . . .	. . . don't buy it.
Take deep breaths . . .	. . . don't hyperventilate.
Exercise . . .	. . . don't tear a ligament.
Play on the swings in the park . . .	. . . don't get on until you've tested to see that the swing will hold your weight.
Update your Rolodex . . .	. . . don't throw away the old cards.
Ask questions about everything . . .	. . . don't ask them out loud.
Pay your bills on time . . .	. . . don't forget the postage.
Plan to quit and look for a better job . . .	. . . don't do it yet.

During MR you should . . .	But . . .
Apologize . . .	. . . don't make excuses.
Be tolerant . . .	. . . don't tolerate intolerance.
Meditate on your shortcomings . . .	. . . don't worry about them.
Give thanks for the lessons of unhappy events . . .	. . . don't forget there are two sides to everything.
Use common sense . . .	. . . don't be afraid to enjoy a little common nonsense now and then.
Go to dinner with a friend . . .	. . . don't chew over old arguments.
Make a wish . . .	. . . don't ask for something you don't want.
Practice Tae Bo . . .	. . . don't neglect to warm up first.
Go hiking . . .	. . . don't forget your compass and water bottle.
Expect the unexpected . . .	. . . don't be surprised when the unexpected happens.
Reflect on your day . . .	. . . don't repeat the bad parts.
Play with the dog . . .	. . . don't neglect the cat.
Plan to be fifteen minutes early to appointments . . .	. . . don't be surprised if you're fifteen minutes late.

During MR you should . . .   *But . . .*

When packing to go to Alaska, take a swim suit . . .	. . . don't be surprised if your plane is rerouted to Florida.
Thank store clerks for their help . . .	. . . don't hold up the line.
Examine yourself honestly . . .	. . . don't criticize others.
Visit a body of water— lake, river, ocean . . .	. . . don't drown.
Make resolutions . . .	. . . don't be too hard on yourself if you break them.
Get a checkup at the doctor's . . .	. . . don't tell everyone what you learned.
Plant seeds . . .	. . . don't forget that weeds are living things, too.
Give thanks for the beauty of nature . . .	. . . don't curse when it rains after you've washed the car.
Write a love letter to an old flame . . .	. . . don't you dare send it.
Buy a lottery ticket . . .	. . . don't spend your winnings until you win them.
Repair your old clothes . . .	. . . don't buy new ones.
Slow down . . .	. . . don't rush.
Count your blessings . . .	. . . don't lose track of the list.
Take a nap . . .	. . . don't forget to wake up.

A FINAL WORD

As an astrologer, I know the universe guides us if we learn how to listen to its messages. When the planet Mercury goes retrograde, our communication systems seem to crumble. Rather than seeing these as times of disaster, we can regard them as a chance to discover new ways of thinking and acting.

The benefit of the MR effect is that we can explore the ways we communicate—with ourselves, with other people, with our world. Rather than taking in new information or seeking new experiences, we can devote energy to absorbing the information we already have. We can look back and see how we got to the place where we stand now.

MR is an illusion—the planet never really moves backward. That's an important lesson, too; it reminds us that we humans never stop moving forward in our path to fulfillment. But by taking a step back for a little while every so often, we can choose to move in new and healthier directions, feeling better about ourselves and where we're going; choosing always to move onward and upward in our evolution toward ever greater experience and wisdom.

APPENDIX 7

Mercury's Place in the Heavens: One-Hundred-Year Ephemeris

This table allows you to look up your date of birth (or any other date between 1910 and 2010) and see whether Mercury was direct or retrograde. You can also determine which sign of the Zodiac Mercury was in at the time.

How to Use the Mercury Ephemeris

1. Find your year of birth, located at the top of each section.

2. If you do not see your actual birthday listed, look at the date *before* your birthday. This will tell you the sign your natal Mercury is in and also whether it is retrograde or direct.

For reasons of space, I have not listed every single day in the ephemeris—only the days when Mercury changes signs or direction. For example, the date April 18, 1950, is not listed. Instead, look at the date given before it—in this case, April 8—and you will see that Mercury was direct and in the sign of Taurus. These conditions persisted until the next given date.

3. Refer to chapters 3 and 4 for the qualities associated with your Mercury sign.

MERCURY EPHEMERIS
1910–2010

Date	Motion	Sign
1910		
Jan 3	direct	Aquarius
Jan 17	retrograde	Aquarius
Jan 31	retrograde	Capricorn
Feb 7	direct	Capricorn
Feb 15	direct	Aquarius
Mar 11	direct	Pisces
Mar 29	direct	Aries
Apr 12	direct	Taurus
Apr 30	direct	Gemini
May 13	retrograde	Gemini
Jun 1	retrograde	Taurus
Jun 6	direct	Taurus

Date	Motion	Sign
Jun 11	direct	Gemini
Jul 6	direct	Cancer
Jul 21	direct	Leo
Aug 5	direct	Virgo
Aug 27	direct	Libra
Sep 13	retrograde	Libra
Sep 28	retrograde	Virgo
Oct 5	direct	Virgo
Oct 11	direct	Libra
Oct 31	direct	Scorpio
Nov 19	direct	Sagittarius
Dec 8	direct	Capricorn

1911

Jan 1	retrograde	Capricorn
Jan 21	direct	Capricorn
Feb 12	direct	Aquarius
Mar 4	direct	Pisces
Mar 20	direct	Aries
Apr 5	direct	Taurus
Apr 24	retrograde	Taurus
May 18	direct	Taurus
Jun 12	direct	Gemini
Jun 28	direct	Cancer
Jul 12	direct	Leo
Jul 30	direct	Virgo
Aug 26	retrograde	Virgo
Sep 18	direct	Virgo
Oct 6	direct	Libra

Date	Motion	Sign
Oct 24	direct	Scorpio
Nov 11	direct	Sagittarius
Dec 2	direct	Capricorn
Dec 16	retrograde	Capricorn
Dec 27	retrograde	Sagittarius

1912

Jan 4	direct	Sagittarius
Jan 14	direct	Capricorn
Feb 6	direct	Aquarius
Feb 24	direct	Pisces
Mar 11	direct	Aries
Apr 5	retrograde	Aries
Apr 28	direct	Aries
May 16	direct	Taurus
Jun 4	direct	Gemini
Jun 19	direct	Cancer
Jul 4	direct	Leo
Jul 26	direct	Virgo
Aug 8	retrograde	Virgo
Aug 20	retrograde	Leo
Aug 31	direct	Leo
Sep 10	direct	Virgo
Sep 28	direct	Libra
Oct 15	direct	Scorpio
Nov 4	direct	Sagittarius
Nov 28	retrograde	Sagittarius
Dec 18	direct	Sagittarius

Date	Motion	Sign
1913		
Jan 9	direct	Capricorn
Jan 29	direct	Aquarius
Feb 16	direct	Pisces
Mar 4	direct	Aries
Mar 18	retrograde	Aries
Apr 9	retrograde	Pisces
Apr 10	direct	Pisces
Apr 13	direct	Aries
May 12	direct	Taurus
May 27	direct	Gemini
Jun 10	direct	Cancer
Jun 28	direct	Leo
Jul 21	retrograde	Leo
Aug 14	direct	Leo
Sep 4	direct	Virgo
Sep 20	direct	Libra
Oct 8	direct	Scorpio
Oct 30	direct	Sagittarius
Nov 12	retrograde	Sagittarius
Nov 23	retrograde	Scorpio
Dec 2	direct	Scorpio
Dec 13	direct	Sagittarius
1914		
Jan 3	direct	Capricorn
Jan 22	direct	Aquarius

Date	Motion	Sign
Feb 8	direct	Pisces
Mar 1	retrograde	Pisces
Mar 23	direct	Pisces
Apr 16	direct	Aries
May 4	direct	Taurus
May 19	direct	Gemini
Jun 3	direct	Cancer
Jul 3	retrograde	Cancer
Jul 27	direct	Cancer
Aug 10	direct	Leo
Aug 27	direct	Virgo
Sep 12	direct	Libra
Oct 2	direct	Scorpio
Oct 27	retrograde	Scorpio
Nov 16	direct	Scorpio
Dec 7	direct	Sagittarius
Dec 27	direct	Capricorn

1915

Jan 14	direct	Aquarius
Feb 2	direct	Pisces
Feb 12	retrograde	Pisces
Feb 23	retrograde	Aquarius
Mar 6	direct	Aquarius
Mar 19	direct	Pisces
Apr 10	direct	Aries
Apr 26	direct	Taurus
May 10	direct	Gemini
May 29	direct	Cancer

Date	Motion	Sign
Jun 14	retrograde	Cancer
Jul 8	direct	Cancer
Aug 4	direct	Leo
Aug 18	direct	Virgo
Sep 5	direct	Libra
Sep 28	direct	Scorpio
Oct 10	retrograde	Scorpio
Oct 20	retrograde	Libra
Oct 31	direct	Libra
Nov 11	direct	Scorpio
Dec 1	direct	Sagittarius
Dec 20	direct	Capricorn

1916

Date	Motion	Sign
Jan 7	direct	Aquarius
Jan 27	retrograde	Aquarius
Feb 17	direct	Aquarius
Mar 14	direct	Pisces
Apr 2	direct	Aries
Apr 17	direct	Taurus
May 2	direct	Gemini
May 24	retrograde	Gemini
Jun 17	direct	Gemini
Jul 10	direct	Cancer
Jul 25	direct	Leo
Aug 9	direct	Virgo
Aug 28	direct	Libra
Sep 22	retrograde	Libra
Oct 14	direct	Libra

Date	Motion	Sign
Nov 4	direct	Scorpio
Nov 22	direct	Sagittarius
Dec 12	direct	Capricorn

1917

Date	Motion	Sign
Jan 1	direct	Aquarius
Jan 10	retrograde	Aquarius
Jan 17	retrograde	Capricorn
Jan 30	direct	Capricorn
Feb 14	direct	Aquarius
Mar 8	direct	Pisces
Mar 25	direct	Aries
Apr 9	direct	Taurus
May 5	retrograde	Taurus
May 29	direct	Taurus
Jun 14	direct	Gemini
Jul 3	direct	Cancer
Jul 17	direct	Leo
Aug 2	direct	Virgo
Aug 26	direct	Libra
Sep 5	retrograde	Libra
Sep 14	retrograde	Virgo
Sep 27	direct	Virgo
Oct 9	direct	Libra
Oct 27	direct	Scorpio
Nov 15	direct	Sagittarius
Dec 5	direct	Capricorn
Dec 24	retrograde	Capricorn

Date	Motion	Sign
1918		
Jan 14	direct	Capricorn
Feb 10	direct	Aquarius
Mar 1	direct	Pisces
Mar 17	direct	Aries
Apr 2	direct	Taurus
Apr 16	retrograde	Taurus
May 10	direct	Taurus
Jun 9	direct	Gemini
Jun 24	direct	Cancer
Jul 9	direct	Leo
Jul 27	direct	Virgo
Aug 19	retrograde	Virgo
Sep 11	direct	Virgo
Oct 3	direct	Libra
Oct 20	direct	Scorpio
Nov 8	direct	Sagittarius
Dec 1	direct	Capricorn
Dec 8	retrograde	Capricorn
Dec 14	retrograde	Sagittarius
Dec 28	direct	Sagittarius
1919		
Jan 13	direct	Capricorn
Feb 3	direct	Aquarius
Feb 21	direct	Pisces
Mar 9	direct	Aries

Date	Motion	Sign
Mar 29	retrograde	Aries
Apr 21	direct	Aries
May 15	direct	Taurus
Jun 2	direct	Gemini
Jun 16	direct	Cancer
Jul 1	direct	Leo
Aug 1	retrograde	Leo
Aug 25	direct	Leo
Sep 8	direct	Virgo
Sep 25	direct	Libra
Oct 13	direct	Scorpio
Nov 2	direct	Sagittarius
Nov 22	retrograde	Sagittarius
Dec 12	direct	Sagittarius

1920

Date	Motion	Sign
Jan 7	direct	Capricorn
Jan 27	direct	Aquarius
Feb 13	direct	Pisces
Mar 2	direct	Aries
Mar 10	retrograde	Aries
Mar 19	retrograde	Pisces
Apr 2	direct	Pisces
Apr 17	direct	Aries
May 8	direct	Taurus
May 23	direct	Gemini
Jun 6	direct	Cancer
Jun 26	direct	Leo
Jul 13	retrograde	Leo

Date	Motion	Sign
Aug 3	retrograde	Cancer
Aug 6	direct	Cancer
Aug 9	direct	Leo
Aug 31	direct	Virgo
Sep 16	direct	Libra
Oct 5	direct	Scorpio
Oct 30	direct	Sagittarius
Nov 5	retrograde	Sagittarius
Nov 9	retrograde	Scorpio
Nov 25	direct	Scorpio
Dec 10	direct	Sagittarius
Dec 31	direct	Capricorn

1921

Date	Motion	Sign
Jan 18	direct	Aquarius
Feb 5	direct	Pisces
Feb 21	retrograde	Pisces
Mar 16	direct	Pisces
Apr 13	direct	Aries
May 1	direct	Taurus
May 15	direct	Gemini
May 31	direct	Cancer
Jun 24	retrograde	Cancer
Jul 18	direct	Cancer
Aug 8	direct	Leo
Aug 23	direct	Virgo
Sep 8	direct	Libra
Sep 29	direct	Scorpio
Oct 19	retrograde	Scorpio

Date	Motion	Sign
Nov 9	direct	Scorpio
Dec 4	direct	Sagittarius
Dec 24	direct	Capricorn

1922

Date	Motion	Sign
Jan 11	direct	Aquarius
Feb 1	direct	Pisces
Feb 5	retrograde	Pisces
Feb 6	retrograde	Aquarius
Feb 26	direct	Aquarius
Mar 17	direct	Pisces
Apr 7	direct	Aries
Apr 22	direct	Taurus
May 7	direct	Gemini
Jun 1	direct	Cancer
Jun 5	retrograde	Cancer
Jun 9	retrograde	Gemini
Jun 29	direct	Gemini
Jul 13	direct	Cancer
Jul 31	direct	Leo
Aug 15	direct	Virgo
Sep 1	direct	Libra
Oct 3	retrograde	Libra
Oct 24	direct	Libra
Nov 8	direct	Scorpio
Nov 27	direct	Sagittarius
Dec 16	direct	Capricorn

Date	Motion	Sign
1923		
Jan 4	direct	Aquarius
Jan 19	retrograde	Aquarius
Feb 7	retrograde	Capricorn
Feb 9	direct	Capricorn
Feb 13	direct	Aquarius
Mar 12	direct	Pisces
Mar 30	direct	Aries
Apr 14	direct	Taurus
May 1	direct	Gemini
May 17	retrograde	Gemini
Jun 10	direct	Gemini
Jul 8	direct	Cancer
Jul 22	direct	Leo
Aug 7	direct	Virgo
Aug 27	direct	Libra
Sep 16	retrograde	Libra
Oct 4	retrograde	Virgo
Oct 7	direct	Virgo
Oct 11	direct	Libra
Nov 1	direct	Scorpio
Nov 20	direct	Sagittarius
Dec 9	direct	Capricorn
1924		
Jan 3	retrograde	Capricorn
Jan 24	direct	Capricorn

Date	Motion	Sign
Feb 13	direct	Aquarius
Mar 4	direct	Pisces
Mar 21	direct	Aries
Apr 5	direct	Taurus
Apr 26	retrograde	Taurus
May 20	direct	Taurus
Jun 12	direct	Gemini
Jun 29	direct	Cancer
Jul 13	direct	Leo
Jul 30	direct	Virgo
Aug 28	retrograde	Virgo
Sep 20	direct	Virgo
Oct 6	direct	Libra
Oct 24	direct	Scorpio
Nov 12	direct	Sagittarius
Dec 2	direct	Capricorn
Dec 17	retrograde	Capricorn
Dec 31	retrograde	Sagittarius

1925

Date	Motion	Sign
Jan 6	direct	Sagittarius
Jan 13	direct	Capricorn
Feb 7	direct	Aquarius
Feb 25	direct	Pisces
Mar 13	direct	Aries
Apr 1	direct	Taurus
Apr 8	retrograde	Taurus
Apr 15	retrograde	Aries
May 1	direct	Aries

Date	Motion	Sign
May 16	direct	Taurus
Jun 6	direct	Gemini
Jun 20	direct	Cancer
Jul 5	direct	Leo
Jul 26	direct	Virgo
Aug 11	retrograde	Virgo
Aug 27	retrograde	Leo
Sep 3	direct	Leo
Sep 10	direct	Virgo
Sep 29	direct	Libra
Oct 16	direct	Scorpio
Nov 5	direct	Sagittarius
Dec 1	retrograde	Sagittarius
Dec 21	direct	Sagittarius

1926

Date	Motion	Sign
Jan 11	direct	Capricorn
Jan 31	direct	Aquarius
Feb 17	direct	Pisces
Mar 5	direct	Aries
Mar 21	retrograde	Aries
Apr 13	direct	Aries
May 13	direct	Taurus
May 29	direct	Gemini
Jun 12	direct	Cancer
Jun 29	direct	Leo
Jul 24	retrograde	Leo
Aug 17	direct	Leo
Sep 5	direct	Virgo

Date	Motion	Sign
Sep 21	direct	Libra
Oct 9	direct	Scorpio
Oct 31	direct	Sagittarius
Nov 15	retrograde	Sagittarius
Nov 28	retrograde	Scorpio
Dec 5	direct	Scorpio
Dec 13	direct	Sagittarius

1927

Date	Motion	Sign
Jan 4	direct	Capricorn
Jan 23	direct	Aquarius
Feb 9	direct	Pisces
Mar 4	retrograde	Pisces
Mar 26	direct	Pisces
Apr 17	direct	Aries
May 6	direct	Taurus
May 20	direct	Gemini
Jun 4	direct	Cancer
Jun 28	direct	Leo
Jul 6	retrograde	Leo
Jul 13	retrograde	Cancer
Jul 30	direct	Cancer
Aug 11	direct	Leo
Aug 28	direct	Virgo
Sep 13	direct	Libra
Oct 3	direct	Scorpio
Oct 29	retrograde	Scorpio
Nov 19	direct	Scorpio
Dec 9	direct	Sagittarius
Dec 28	direct	Capricorn

Date	Motion	Sign
1928		
Jan 16	direct	Aquarius
Feb 3	direct	Pisces
Feb 15	retrograde	Pisces
Feb 29	retrograde	Aquarius
Mar 8	direct	Aquarius
Mar 17	direct	Pisces
Apr 10	direct	Aries
Apr 27	direct	Taurus
May 11	direct	Gemini
May 28	direct	Cancer
Jun 16	retrograde	Cancer
Jul 10	direct	Cancer
Aug 4	direct	Leo
Aug 19	direct	Virgo
Sep 5	direct	Libra
Sep 27	direct	Scorpio
Oct 12	retrograde	Scorpio
Oct 24	retrograde	Libra
Nov 2	direct	Libra
Nov 10	direct	Scorpio
Dec 1	direct	Sagittarius
Dec 20	direct	Capricorn
1929		
Jan 8	direct	Aquarius
Jan 28	retrograde	Aquarius
Feb 19	direct	Aquarius

Date	Motion	Sign
Mar 15	direct	Pisces
Apr 3	direct	Aries
Apr 18	direct	Taurus
May 3	direct	Gemini
May 28	retrograde	Gemini
Jun 21	direct	Gemini
Jul 11	direct	Cancer
Jul 27	direct	Leo
Aug 11	direct	Virgo
Aug 30	direct	Libra
Sep 25	retrograde	Libra
Oct 16	direct	Libra
Nov 5	direct	Scorpio
Nov 24	direct	Sagittarius
Dec 13	direct	Capricorn

1930

Date	Motion	Sign
Jan 2	direct	Aquarius
Jan 12	retrograde	Aquarius
Jan 22	retrograde	Capricorn
Feb 2	direct	Capricorn
Feb 15	direct	Aquarius
Mar 9	direct	Pisces
Mar 26	direct	Aries
Apr 10	direct	Taurus
May 1	direct	Gemini
May 8	retrograde	Gemini
May 17	retrograde	Taurus
Jun 1	direct	Taurus

Date	Motion	Sign
Jun 14	direct	Gemini
Jul 4	direct	Cancer
Jul 18	direct	Leo
Aug 3	direct	Virgo
Aug 26	direct	Libra
Sep 8	retrograde	Libra
Sep 19	retrograde	Virgo
Sep 30	direct	Virgo
Oct 10	direct	Libra
Oct 29	direct	Scorpio
Nov 16	direct	Sagittarius
Dec 6	direct	Capricorn
Dec 27	retrograde	Capricorn

1931

Date	Motion	Sign
Jan 16	direct	Capricorn
Feb 11	direct	Aquarius
Mar 2	direct	Pisces
Mar 18	direct	Aries
Apr 3	direct	Taurus
Apr 19	retrograde	Taurus
May 13	direct	Taurus
Jun 11	direct	Gemini
Jun 26	direct	Cancer
Jul 10	direct	Leo
Jul 28	direct	Virgo
Aug 22	retrograde	Virgo
Sep 14	direct	Virgo
Oct 4	direct	Libra

Date	Motion	Sign
Oct 21	direct	Scorpio
Nov 9	direct	Sagittarius
Dec 1	direct	Capricorn
Dec 11	retrograde	Capricorn
Dec 19	retrograde	Sagittarius
Dec 31	direct	Sagittarius

1932

Jan 14	direct	Capricorn
Feb 4	direct	Aquarius
Feb 22	direct	Pisces
Mar 9	direct	Aries
Mar 31	retrograde	Aries
Apr 23	direct	Aries
May 15	direct	Taurus
Jun 2	direct	Gemini
Jun 16	direct	Cancer
Jul 2	direct	Leo
Jul 28	direct	Virgo
Aug 3	retrograde	Virgo
Aug 9	retrograde	Leo
Aug 27	direct	Leo
Sep 8	direct	Virgo
Sep 25	direct	Libra
Oct 13	direct	Scorpio
Nov 2	direct	Sagittarius
Nov 24	retrograde	Sagittarius
Dec 14	direct	Sagittarius

Date	Motion	Sign
1933		
Jan 8	direct	Capricorn
Jan 27	direct	Aquarius
Feb 13	direct	Pisces
Mar 3	direct	Aries
Mar 13	retrograde	Aries
Mar 25	retrograde	Pisces
Apr 5	direct	Pisces
Apr 17	direct	Aries
May 10	direct	Taurus
May 25	direct	Gemini
Jun 8	direct	Cancer
Jun 26	direct	Leo
Jul 16	retrograde	Leo
Aug 9	direct	Leo
Sep 1	direct	Virgo
Sep 17	direct	Libra
Oct 6	direct	Scorpio
Oct 30	direct	Sagittarius
Nov 8	retrograde	Sagittarius
Nov 15	retrograde	Scorpio
Nov 28	direct	Scorpio
Dec 11	direct	Sagittarius
1934		
Jan 1	direct	Capricorn
Jan 20	direct	Aquarius

Date	Motion	Sign
Feb 6	direct	Pisces
Feb 24	retrograde	Pisces
Mar 19	direct	Pisces
Apr 14	direct	Aries
May 2	direct	Taurus
May 16	direct	Gemini
Jun 1	direct	Cancer
Jun 27	retrograde	Cancer
Jul 22	direct	Cancer
Aug 9	direct	Leo
Aug 24	direct	Virgo
Sep 10	direct	Libra
Sep 30	direct	Scorpio
Oct 22	retrograde	Scorpio
Nov 11	direct	Scorpio
Dec 6	direct	Sagittarius
Dec 25	direct	Capricorn

1935

Date	Motion	Sign
Jan 12	direct	Aquarius
Feb 1	direct	Pisces
Feb 8	retrograde	Pisces
Feb 14	retrograde	Aquarius
Mar 1	direct	Aquarius
Mar 18	direct	Pisces
Apr 8	direct	Aries
Apr 24	direct	Taurus
May 8	direct	Gemini
May 29	direct	Cancer

Date	Motion	Sign
Jun 8	retrograde	Cancer
Jun 20	retrograde	Gemini
Jul 3	direct	Gemini
Jul 13	direct	Cancer
Aug 1	direct	Leo
Aug 16	direct	Virgo
Sep 3	direct	Libra
Sep 28	direct	Scorpio
Oct 5	retrograde	Scorpio
Oct 11	retrograde	Libra
Oct 26	direct	Libra
Nov 9	direct	Scorpio
Nov 29	direct	Sagittarius
Dec 18	direct	Capricorn

1936

Date	Motion	Sign
Jan 5	direct	Aquarius
Jan 22	retrograde	Aquarius
Feb 12	direct	Aquarius
Mar 12	direct	Pisces
Mar 30	direct	Aries
Apr 14	direct	Taurus
Apr 30	direct	Gemini
May 19	retrograde	Gemini
Jun 12	direct	Gemini
Jul 8	direct	Cancer
Jul 23	direct	Leo
Aug 7	direct	Virgo
Aug 27	direct	Libra

Date	Motion	Sign
Sep 17	retrograde	Libra
Oct 9	direct	Libra
Nov 2	direct	Scorpio
Nov 20	direct	Sagittarius
Dec 10	direct	Capricorn

1937

Date	Motion	Sign
Jan 2	direct	Aquarius
Jan 5	retrograde	Aquarius
Jan 8	retrograde	Capricorn
Jan 26	direct	Capricorn
Feb 13	direct	Aquarius
Mar 6	direct	Pisces
Mar 22	direct	Aries
Apr 6	direct	Taurus
Apr 30	retrograde	Taurus
May 24	direct	Taurus
Jun 13	direct	Gemini
Jun 30	direct	Cancer
Jul 14	direct	Leo
Jul 31	direct	Virgo
Aug 31	retrograde	Virgo
Sep 23	direct	Virgo
Oct 8	direct	Libra
Oct 25	direct	Scorpio
Nov 13	direct	Sagittarius
Dec 3	direct	Capricorn
Dec 20	retrograde	Capricorn

Date	Motion	Sign
1938		
Jan 9	retrograde	Sagittarius
Jan 9	direct	Sagittarius
Jan 11	direct	Capricorn
Feb 8	direct	Aquarius
Feb 26	direct	Pisces
Mar 14	direct	Aries
Apr 1	direct	Taurus
Apr 11	retrograde	Taurus
Apr 23	retrograde	Aries
May 5	direct	Aries
May 16	direct	Taurus
Jun 7	direct	Gemini
Jun 22	direct	Cancer
Jul 6	direct	Leo
Jul 26	direct	Virgo
Aug 14	retrograde	Virgo
Sep 5	retrograde	Leo
Sep 6	direct	Leo
Sep 9	direct	Virgo
Sep 30	direct	Libra
Oct 18	direct	Scorpio
Nov 6	direct	Sagittarius
Dec 4	retrograde	Sagittarius
Dec 24	direct	Sagittarius

Date	Motion	Sign
1939		
Jan 12	direct	Capricorn
Feb 1	direct	Aquarius
Feb 19	direct	Pisces
Mar 7	direct	Aries
Mar 24	retrograde	Aries
Apr 16	direct	Aries
May 14	direct	Taurus
May 30	direct	Gemini
Jun 13	direct	Cancer
Jun 30	direct	Leo
Jul 27	retrograde	Leo
Aug 20	direct	Leo
Sep 6	direct	Virgo
Sep 23	direct	Libra
Oct 10	direct	Scorpio
Nov 1	direct	Sagittarius
Nov 18	retrograde	Sagittarius
Dec 4	retrograde	Scorpio
Dec 8	direct	Scorpio
Dec 13	direct	Sagittarius
1940		
Jan 6	direct	Capricorn
Jan 25	direct	Aquarius
Feb 11	direct	Pisces
Mar 5	retrograde	Pisces

Date	Motion	Sign
Mar 28	direct	Pisces
Apr 16	direct	Aries
May 6	direct	Taurus
May 21	direct	Gemini
Jun 4	direct	Cancer
Jun 26	direct	Leo
Jul 8	retrograde	Leo
Jul 20	retrograde	Cancer
Aug 1	direct	Cancer
Aug 11	direct	Leo
Aug 29	direct	Virgo
Sep 14	direct	Libra
Oct 3	direct	Scorpio
Oct 31	retrograde	Scorpio
Nov 20	direct	Scorpio
Dec 9	direct	Sagittarius
Dec 29	direct	Capricorn

1941

Jan 16	direct	Aquarius
Feb 3	direct	Pisces
Feb 17	retrograde	Pisces
Mar 7	retrograde	Aquarius
Mar 11	direct	Aquarius
Mar 15	direct	Pisces
Apr 12	direct	Aries
Apr 28	direct	Taurus
May 12	direct	Gemini
May 29	direct	Cancer

Date	Motion	Sign
Jun 19	retrograde	Cancer
Jul 13	direct	Cancer
Aug 5	direct	Leo
Aug 20	direct	Virgo
Sep 6	direct	Libra
Sep 28	direct	Scorpio
Oct 15	retrograde	Scorpio
Oct 29	retrograde	Libra
Nov 4	direct	Libra
Nov 11	direct	Scorpio
Dec 2	direct	Sagittarius
Dec 21	direct	Capricorn

1942

Date	Motion	Sign
Jan 9	direct	Aquarius
Jan 31	retrograde	Aquarius
Feb 22	direct	Aquarius
Mar 16	direct	Pisces
Apr 5	direct	Aries
Apr 20	direct	Taurus
May 5	direct	Gemini
May 31	retrograde	Gemini
Jun 24	direct	Gemini
Jul 12	direct	Cancer
Jul 28	direct	Leo
Aug 12	direct	Virgo
Aug 31	direct	Libra
Sep 28	retrograde	Libra
Oct 19	direct	Libra

Date	Motion	Sign
Nov 6	direct	Scorpio
Nov 25	direct	Sagittarius
Dec 14	direct	Capricorn

1943

Jan 3	direct	Aquarius
Jan 15	retrograde	Aquarius
Jan 27	retrograde	Capricorn
Feb 5	direct	Capricorn
Feb 15	direct	Aquarius
Mar 10	direct	Pisces
Mar 28	direct	Aries
Apr 11	direct	Taurus
Apr 30	direct	Gemini
May 11	retrograde	Gemini
May 26	retrograde	Taurus
Jun 4	direct	Taurus
Jun 13	direct	Gemini
Jul 6	direct	Cancer
Jul 20	direct	Leo
Aug 5	direct	Virgo
Aug 26	direct	Libra
Sep 11	retrograde	Libra
Sep 25	retrograde	Virgo
Oct 3	direct	Virgo
Oct 11	direct	Libra
Oct 30	direct	Scorpio
Nov 18	direct	Sagittarius

Date	Motion	Sign
Dec 7	direct	Capricorn
Dec 30	retrograde	Capricorn

1944

Jan 19	direct	Capricorn
Feb 12	direct	Aquarius
Mar 2	direct	Pisces
Mar 19	direct	Aries
Apr 3	direct	Taurus
Apr 21	retrograde	Taurus
May 15	direct	Taurus
Jun 11	direct	Gemini
Jun 26	direct	Cancer
Jul 11	direct	Leo
Jul 28	direct	Virgo
Aug 24	retrograde	Virgo
Sep 16	direct	Virgo
Oct 4	direct	Libra
Oct 22	direct	Scorpio
Nov 10	direct	Sagittarius
Dec 1	direct	Capricorn
Dec 13	retrograde	Capricorn
Dec 24	retrograde	Sagittarius

1945

Jan 2	direct	Sagittarius
Jan 13	direct	Capricorn
Feb 5	direct	Aquarius

Date	Motion	Sign
Feb 23	direct	Pisces
Mar 11	direct	Aries
Apr 3	retrograde	Aries
Apr 26	direct	Aries
May 16	direct	Taurus
Jun 4	direct	Gemini
Jun 18	direct	Cancer
Jul 3	direct	Leo
Jul 26	direct	Virgo
Aug 6	retrograde	Virgo
Aug 17	retrograde	Leo
Aug 30	direct	Leo
Sep 10	direct	Virgo
Sep 27	direct	Libra
Oct 14	direct	Scorpio
Nov 3	direct	Sagittarius
Nov 27	retrograde	Sagittarius
Dec 17	direct	Sagittarius

1946

Date	Motion	Sign
Jan 9	direct	Capricorn
Jan 29	direct	Aquarius
Feb 15	direct	Pisces
Mar 4	direct	Aries
Mar 16	retrograde	Aries
Apr 2	retrograde	Pisces
Apr 8	direct	Pisces
Apr 16	direct	Aries
May 11	direct	Taurus

Date	Motion	Sign
May 26	direct	Gemini
Jun 9	direct	Cancer
Jun 27	direct	Leo
Jul 19	retrograde	Leo
Aug 12	direct	Leo
Sep 3	direct	Virgo
Sep 19	direct	Libra
Oct 7	direct	Scorpio
Oct 30	direct	Sagittarius
Nov 10	retrograde	Sagittarius
Nov 20	retrograde	Scorpio
Nov 30	direct	Scorpio
Dec 12	direct	Sagittarius

1947

Date	Motion	Sign
Jan 2	direct	Capricorn
Jan 21	direct	Aquarius
Feb 7	direct	Pisces
Feb 27	retrograde	Pisces
Mar 22	direct	Pisces
Apr 15	direct	Aries
May 3	direct	Taurus
May 18	direct	Gemini
Jun 2	direct	Cancer
Jul 1	retrograde	Cancer
Jul 25	direct	Cancer
Aug 10	direct	Leo
Aug 26	direct	Virgo
Sep 11	direct	Libra

Date	Motion	Sign
Oct 1	direct	Scorpio
Oct 25	retrograde	Scorpio
Nov 14	direct	Scorpio
Dec 7	direct	Sagittarius
Dec 26	direct	Capricorn

1948

Date	Motion	Sign
Jan 14	direct	Aquarius
Feb 1	direct	Pisces
Feb 10	retrograde	Pisces
Feb 20	retrograde	Aquarius
Mar 3	direct	Aquarius
Mar 18	direct	Pisces
Apr 8	direct	Aries
Apr 24	direct	Taurus
May 8	direct	Gemini
May 28	direct	Cancer
Jun 11	retrograde	Cancer
Jun 29	retrograde	Gemini
Jul 5	direct	Gemini
Jul 11	direct	Cancer
Aug 2	direct	Leo
Aug 17	direct	Virgo
Sep 3	direct	Libra
Sep 27	direct	Scorpio
Oct 7	retrograde	Scorpio
Oct 16	retrograde	Libra
Oct 28	direct	Libra
Nov 9	direct	Scorpio

Date	Motion	Sign
Nov 29	direct	Sagittarius
Dec 18	direct	Capricorn

1949

Date	Motion	Sign
Jan 6	direct	Aquarius
Jan 24	retrograde	Aquarius
Feb 14	direct	Aquarius
Mar 14	direct	Pisces
Apr 1	direct	Aries
Apr 16	direct	Taurus
May 1	direct	Gemini
May 22	retrograde	Gemini
Jun 15	direct	Gemini
Jul 9	direct	Cancer
Jul 24	direct	Leo
Aug 9	direct	Virgo
Aug 28	direct	Libra
Sep 20	retrograde	Libra
Oct 12	direct	Libra
Nov 3	direct	Scorpio
Nov 22	direct	Sagittarius
Dec 11	direct	Capricorn

1950

Date	Motion	Sign
Jan 1	direct	Aquarius
Jan 8	retrograde	Aquarius
Jan 14	retrograde	Capricorn
Jan 28	direct	Capricorn

Date	Motion	Sign
Feb 14	direct	Aquarius
Mar 7	direct	Pisces
Mar 24	direct	Aries
Apr 8	direct	Taurus
May 3	retrograde	Taurus
May 27	direct	Taurus
Jun 14	direct	Gemini
Jul 2	direct	Cancer
Jul 16	direct	Leo
Aug 1	direct	Virgo
Aug 27	direct	Libra
Sep 3	retrograde	Libra
Sep 9	retrograde	Virgo
Sep 26	direct	Virgo
Oct 9	direct	Libra
Oct 27	direct	Scorpio
Nov 14	direct	Sagittarius
Dec 4	direct	Capricorn
Dec 23	retrograde	Capricorn

1951

Jan 12	direct	Capricorn
Feb 9	direct	Aquarius
Feb 28	direct	Pisces
Mar 16	direct	Aries
Apr 1	direct	Taurus
Apr 14	retrograde	Taurus
May 2	retrograde	Aries
May 8	direct	Aries

Date	Motion	Sign
May 14	direct	Taurus
Jun 9	direct	Gemini
Jun 23	direct	Cancer
Jul 8	direct	Leo
Jul 27	direct	Virgo
Aug 17	retrograde	Virgo
Sep 9	direct	Virgo
Oct 2	direct	Libra
Oct 19	direct	Scorpio
Nov 7	direct	Sagittarius
Dec 1	direct	Capricorn
Dec 7	retrograde	Capricorn
Dec 11	retrograde	Sagittarius
Dec 27	direct	Sagittarius

1952

Date	Motion	Sign
Jan 12	direct	Capricorn
Feb 2	direct	Aquarius
Feb 20	direct	Pisces
Mar 7	direct	Aries
Mar 26	retrograde	Aries
Apr 18	direct	Aries
May 14	direct	Taurus
May 31	direct	Gemini
Jun 14	direct	Cancer
Jun 30	direct	Leo
Jul 29	retrograde	Leo
Aug 22	direct	Leo
Sep 7	direct	Virgo

Date	Motion	Sign
Sep 23	direct	Libra
Oct 11	direct	Scorpio
Nov 1	direct	Sagittarius
Nov 20	retrograde	Sagittarius
Dec 9	direct	Sagittarius

1953

Date	Motion	Sign
Jan 6	direct	Capricorn
Jan 25	direct	Aquarius
Feb 11	direct	Pisces
Mar 2	direct	Aries
Mar 8	retrograde	Aries
Mar 15	retrograde	Pisces
Mar 31	direct	Pisces
Apr 17	direct	Aries
May 7	direct	Taurus
May 22	direct	Gemini
Jun 6	direct	Cancer
Jun 26	direct	Leo
Jul 11	retrograde	Leo
Jul 28	retrograde	Cancer
Aug 4	direct	Cancer
Aug 10	direct	Leo
Aug 30	direct	Virgo
Sep 15	direct	Libra
Oct 4	direct	Scorpio
Nov 3	direct	Sagittarius
Nov 3	retrograde	Sagittarius[a]

[a]Mercury entered Sagittarius on November 3 and went retrograde later that day.

Date	Motion	Sign
Nov 6	retrograde	Scorpio
Nov 23	direct	Scorpio
Dec 10	direct	Sagittarius
Dec 30	direct	Capricorn

1954

Jan 18	direct	Aquarius
Feb 4	direct	Pisces
Feb 20	retrograde	Pisces
Mar 14	direct	Pisces
Apr 13	direct	Aries
Apr 30	direct	Taurus
May 14	direct	Gemini
May 30	direct	Cancer
Jun 24	retrograde	Cancer
Jul 17	direct	Cancer
Aug 7	direct	Leo
Aug 22	direct	Virgo
Sep 8	direct	Libra
Sep 29	direct	Scorpio
Oct 18	retrograde	Scorpio
Nov 7	direct	Scorpio
Dec 4	direct	Sagittarius
Dec 23	direct	Capricorn

1955

Jan 10	direct	Aquarius
Feb 3	retrograde	Aquarius

Date	Motion	Sign
Feb 25	direct	Aquarius
Mar 17	direct	Pisces
Apr 6	direct	Aries
Apr 21	direct	Taurus
May 6	direct	Gemini
Jun 3	retrograde	Gemini
Jun 27	direct	Gemini
Jul 13	direct	Cancer
Jul 30	direct	Leo
Aug 1	direct	Virgo
Sep 1	direct	Libra
Oct 1	retrograde	Libra
Oct 22	direct	Libra
Nov 2	direct	Sagittarius
Nov 8	direct	Scorpio
Dec 1	direct	Capricorn

1956

Date	Motion	Sign
Jan 4	direct	Aquarius
Jan 18	retrograde	Aquarius
Feb 2	retrograde	Capricorn
Feb 8	direct	Capricorn
Feb 15	direct	Aquarius
Mar 11	direct	Pisces
Mar 28	direct	Aries
Apr 1	direct	Taurus
Apr 9	direct	Gemini
May 14	retrograde	Gemini
Jun 7	direct	Gemini

Date	Motion	Sign
Jul 6	direct	Cancer
Jul 21	direct	Leo
Aug 5	direct	Virgo
Aug 26	direct	Libra
Sep 13	retrograde	Libra
Sep 30	retrograde	Virgo
Oct 5	direct	Virgo
Oct 10	direct	Libra
Oct 31	direct	Scorpio
Nov 18	direct	Sagittarius
Dec 8	direct	Capricorn

1957

Jan 1	retrograde	Capricorn
Jan 21	direct	Capricorn
Feb 12	direct	Aquarius
Mar 4	direct	Pisces
Mar 2	direct	Aries
Apr 4	direct	Taurus
Apr 24	retrograde	Taurus
May 18	direct	Taurus
Jun 12	direct	Gemini
Jun 28	direct	Cancer
Jul 12	direct	Leo
Jul 29	direct	Virgo
Aug 27	retrograde	Virgo
Sep 18	direct	Virgo
Oct 6	direct	Libra
Oct 23	direct	Scorpio

Date	Motion	Sign
Nov 11	direct	Sagittarius
Dec 2	direct	Capricorn
Dec 16	retrograde	Capricorn
Dec 29	retrograde	Sagittarius

1958

Jan 5	direct	Sagittarius
Jan 14	direct	Capricorn
Feb 6	direct	Aquarius
Feb 24	direct	Pisces
Mar 12	direct	Aries
Apr 3	direct	Taurus
Apr 6	retrograde	Taurus
Apr 9	retrograde	Aries
Apr 30	direct	Aries
May 1	direct	Taurus
Jun 5	direct	Gemini
Jun 19	direct	Cancer
Jul 4	direct	Leo
Jul 26	direct	Virgo
Aug 9	retrograde	Virgo
Aug 23	retrograde	Leo
Sep 2	direct	Leo
Sep 10	direct	Virgo
Sep 28	direct	Libra
Oct 16	direct	Scorpio
Nov 4	direct	Sagittarius
Nov 30	retrograde	Sagittarius
Dec 19	direct	Sagittarius

Date	Motion	Sign
1959		
Jan 10	direct	Capricorn
Jan 30	direct	Aquarius
Feb 16	direct	Pisces
Mar 5	direct	Aries
Mar 19	retrograde	Aries
Apr 11	direct	Aries
May 12	direct	Taurus
May 28	direct	Gemini
Jun 11	direct	Cancer
Jun 28	direct	Leo
Jul 22	retrograde	Leo
Aug 15	direct	Leo
Sep 4	direct	Virgo
Sep 20	direct	Libra
Oct 8	direct	Scorpio
Oct 30	direct	Sagittarius
Nov 13	retrograde	Sagittarius
Nov 25	retrograde	Scorpio
Dec 3	direct	Scorpio
Dec 13	direct	Sagittarius
1960		
Jan 4	direct	Capricorn
Jan 22	direct	Aquarius
Feb 9	direct	Pisces
Mar 1	retrograde	Pisces
Mar 24	direct	Pisces

Date	Motion	Sign
Apr 15	direct	Aries
May 4	direct	Taurus
May 18	direct	Gemini
Jun 2	direct	Cancer
Jul 3	retrograde	Cancer
Jul 27	direct	Cancer
Aug 10	direct	Leo
Aug 26	direct	Virgo
Sep 12	direct	Libra
Oct 1	direct	Scorpio
Oct 27	retrograde	Scorpio
Nov 16	direct	Scorpio
Dec 7	direct	Sagittarius
Dec 27	direct	Capricorn

1961

Date	Motion	Sign
Jan 14	direct	Aquarius
Feb 1	direct	Pisces
Feb 12	retrograde	Pisces
Feb 24	retrograde	Aquarius
Mar 6	direct	Aquarius
Mar 17	direct	Pisces
Apr 10	direct	Aries
Apr 26	direct	Taurus
May 10	direct	Gemini
May 28	direct	Cancer
Jun 14	retrograde	Cancer
Jul 8	direct	Cancer
Aug 3	direct	Leo

Date	Motion	Sign
Aug 18	direct	Virgo
Sep 4	direct	Libra
Sep 27	direct	Scorpio
Oct 10	retrograde	Scorpio
Oct 21	retrograde	Libra
Oct 31	direct	Libra
Nov 10	direct	Scorpio
Nov 30	direct	Sagittarius
Dec 19	direct	Capricorn

1962

Date	Motion	Sign
Jan 7	direct	Aquarius
Jan 27	retrograde	Aquarius
Feb 17	direct	Aquarius
Mar 15	direct	Pisces
Apr 2	direct	Aries
Apr 17	direct	Taurus
May 3	direct	Gemini
May 26	retrograde	Gemini
Jun 19	direct	Gemini
Jul 10	direct	Cancer
Jul 26	direct	Leo
Aug 10	direct	Virgo
Aug 29	direct	Libra
Sep 23	retrograde	Libra
Oct 15	direct	Libra
Nov 4	direct	Scorpio
Nov 23	direct	Sagittarius
Dec 12	direct	Capricorn

Date	Motion	Sign
1963		
Jan 1	direct	Aquarius
Jan 11	retrograde	Aquarius
Jan 19	retrograde	Capricorn
Jan 31	direct	Capricorn
Feb 15	direct	Aquarius
Mar 8	direct	Pisces
Mar 25	direct	Aries
Apr 9	direct	Taurus
May 3	direct	Gemini
May 6	retrograde	Gemini
May 10	retrograde	Taurus
May 30	direct	Taurus
Jun 14	direct	Gemini
Jul 3	direct	Cancer
Jul 18	direct	Leo
Aug 3	direct	Virgo
Aug 26	direct	Libra
Sep 6	retrograde	Libra
Sep 16	retrograde	Virgo
Sep 29	direct	Virgo
Oct 10	direct	Libra
Oct 28	direct	Scorpio
Nov 16	direct	Sagittarius
Dec 5	direct	Capricorn
Dec 26	retrograde	Capricorn

Date	Motion	Sign
1964		
Jan 15	direct	Capricorn
Feb 10	direct	Aquarius
Feb 29	direct	Pisces
Mar 16	direct	Aries
Apr 1	direct	Taurus
Apr 16	retrograde	Taurus
May 10	direct	Taurus
Jun 9	direct	Gemini
Jun 24	direct	Cancer
Jul 8	direct	Leo
Jul 27	direct	Virgo
Aug 19	retrograde	Virgo
Sep 11	direct	Virgo
Oct 2	direct	Libra
Oct 20	direct	Scorpio
Nov 8	direct	Sagittarius
Nov 30	direct	Capricorn
Dec 9	retrograde	Capricorn
Dec 15	retrograde	Sagittarius
Dec 28	direct	Sagittarius
1965		
Jan 12	direct	Capricorn
Feb 3	direct	Aquarius
Feb 20	direct	Pisces
Mar 8	direct	Aries
Mar 29	retrograde	Aries

Date	Motion	Sign
Apr 21	direct	Aries
May 15	direct	Taurus
Jun 1	direct	Gemini
Jun 15	direct	Cancer
Jul 1	direct	Leo
Aug 1	retrograde	Leo
Aug 25	direct	Leo
Sep 8	direct	Virgo
Sep 24	direct	Libra
Oct 12	direct	Scorpio
Nov 2	direct	Sagittarius
Nov 22	retrograde	Sagittarius
Dec 12	direct	Sagittarius

1966

Jan 7	direct	Capricorn
Jan 26	direct	Aquarius
Feb 13	direct	Pisces
Mar 3	direct	Aries
Mar 11	retrograde	Aries
Mar 21	retrograde	Pisces
Apr 3	direct	Pisces
Apr 17	direct	Aries
May 9	direct	Taurus
May 24	direct	Gemini
Jun 7	direct	Cancer
Jun 26	direct	Leo
Jul 14	retrograde	Leo
Aug 7	direct	Leo

Date	Motion	Sign
Sep 1	direct	Virgo
Sep 17	direct	Libra
Oct 5	direct	Scorpio
Oct 30	direct	Sagittarius
Nov 6	retrograde	Sagittarius
Nov 12	retrograde	Scorpio
Nov 26	direct	Scorpio
Dec 11	direct	Sagittarius
Dec 31	direct	Capricorn

1967

Date	Motion	Sign
Jan 19	direct	Aquarius
Feb 5	direct	Pisces
Feb 22	retrograde	Pisces
Mar 17	direct	Pisces
Apr 14	direct	Aries
May 1	direct	Taurus
May 15	direct	Gemini
May 31	direct	Cancer
Jun 26	retrograde	Cancer
Jul 20	direct	Cancer
Aug 8	direct	Leo
Aug 24	direct	Virgo
Sep 9	direct	Libra
Sep 29	direct	Scorpio
Oct 20	retrograde	Scorpio
Nov 10	direct	Scorpio
Dec 5	direct	Sagittarius
Dec 24	direct	Capricorn

Date	Motion	Sign
1968		
Jan 12	direct	Aquarius
Feb 1	direct	Pisces
Feb 6	retrograde	Pisces
Feb 10	retrograde	Aquarius
Feb 28	direct	Aquarius
Mar 17	direct	Pisces
Apr 6	direct	Aries
Apr 22	direct	Taurus
May 6	direct	Gemini
May 29	direct	Cancer
Jun 5	retrograde	Cancer
Jun 13	retrograde	Gemini
Jun 30	direct	Gemini
Jul 12	direct	Cancer
Jul 31	direct	Leo
Aug 14	direct	Virgo
Sep 1	direct	Libra
Sep 28	direct	Scorpio
Oct 3	retrograde	Scorpio
Oct 6	retrograde	Libra
Oct 24	direct	Libra
Nov 8	direct	Scorpio
Nov 27	direct	Sagittarius
Dec 16	direct	Capricorn
1969		
Jan 4	direct	Aquarius
Jan 20	retrograde	Aquarius

Date	Motion	Sign
Feb 10	direct	Aquarius
Mar 12	direct	Pisces
Mar 30	direct	Aries
Apr 14	direct	Taurus
Apr 30	direct	Gemini
May 17	retrograde	Gemini
Jun 10	direct	Gemini
Jul 7	direct	Cancer
Jul 22	direct	Leo
Aug 6	direct	Virgo
Aug 27	direct	Libra
Sep 16	retrograde	Libra
Oct 8	direct	Libra
Nov 1	direct	Scorpio
Nov 20	direct	Sagittarius
Dec 9	direct	Capricorn

1970

Date	Motion	Sign
Jan 4	retrograde	Capricorn
Jan 24	direct	Capricorn
Feb 13	direct	Aquarius
Mar 5	direct	Pisces
Mar 22	direct	Aries
Apr 6	direct	Taurus
Apr 28	retrograde	Taurus
May 22	direct	Taurus
Jun 13	direct	Gemini
Jun 29	direct	Cancer
Jul 14	direct	Leo

Date	Motion	Sign
Jul 30	direct	Virgo
Aug 30	retrograde	Virgo
Sep 21	direct	Virgo
Oct 7	direct	Libra
Oct 25	direct	Scorpio
Nov 12	direct	Sagittarius
Dec 3	direct	Capricorn
Dec 18	retrograde	Capricorn

1971

Date	Motion	Sign
Jan 4	retrograde	Sagittarius
Jan 7	direct	Sagittarius
Jan 13	direct	Capricorn
Feb 7	direct	Aquarius
Feb 26	direct	Pisces
Mar 13	direct	Aries
Apr 1	direct	Taurus
Apr 9	retrograde	Taurus
Apr 18	retrograde	Aries
May 3	direct	Aries
May 16	direct	Taurus
Jun 6	direct	Gemini
Jun 21	direct	Cancer
Jul 6	direct	Leo
Jul 26	direct	Virgo
Aug 12	retrograde	Virgo
Aug 30	retrograde	Leo
Sep 5	direct	Leo
Sep 10	direct	Virgo

Date	Motion	Sign
Sep 30	direct	Libra
Oct 17	direct	Scorpio
Nov 6	direct	Sagittarius
Dec 2	retrograde	Sagittarius
Dec 22	direct	Sagittarius

1972

Jan 11	direct	Capricorn
Jan 31	direct	Aquarius
Feb 18	direct	Pisces
Mar 5	direct	Aries
Mar 21	retrograde	Aries
Apr 13	direct	Aries
May 12	direct	Taurus
May 28	direct	Gemini
Jun 11	direct	Cancer
Jun 28	direct	Leo
Jul 24	retrograde	Leo
Aug 17	direct	Leo
Sep 5	direct	Virgo
Sep 21	direct	Libra
Oct 9	direct	Scorpio
Oct 30	direct	Sagittarius
Nov 15	retrograde	Sagittarius
Nov 29	retrograde	Scorpio
Dec 5	direct	Scorpio
Dec 12	direct	Sagittarius

Date	Motion	Sign
1973		
Jan 4	direct	Capricorn
Jan 23	direct	Aquarius
Feb 9	direct	Pisces
Mar 4	retrograde	Pisces
Mar 27	direct	Pisces
Apr 16	direct	Aries
May 5	direct	Taurus
May 20	direct	Gemini
Jun 3	direct	Cancer
Jun 27	direct	Leo
Jul 6	retrograde	Leo
Jul 15	retrograde	Cancer
Jul 30	direct	Cancer
Aug 11	direct	Leo
Aug 28	direct	Virgo
Sep 13	direct	Libra
Oct 2	direct	Scorpio
Oct 30	retrograde	Scorpio
Nov 19	direct	Scorpio
Dec 8	direct	Sagittarius
Dec 28	direct	Capricorn
1974		
Jan 15	direct	Aquarius
Feb 2	direct	Pisces
Feb 15	retrograde	Pisces
Mar 3	retrograde	Aquarius

Date	Motion	Sign
Mar 9	direct	Aquarius
Mar 17	direct	Pisces
Apr 11	direct	Aries
Apr 27	direct	Taurus
May 11	direct	Gemini
May 29	direct	Cancer
Jun 17	retrograde	Cancer
Jul 11	direct	Cancer
Aug 5	direct	Leo
Aug 20	direct	Virgo
Sep 6	direct	Libra
Sep 27	direct	Scorpio
Oct 13	retrograde	Scorpio
Oct 27	retrograde	Libra
Nov 3	direct	Libra
Nov 11	direct	Scorpio
Dec 2	direct	Sagittarius
Dec 21	direct	Capricorn

1975

Date	Motion	Sign
Jan 8	direct	Aquarius
Jan 30	retrograde	Aquarius
Feb 20	direct	Aquarius
Mar 16	direct	Pisces
Apr 4	direct	Aries
Apr 19	direct	Taurus
May 4	direct	Gemini
May 29	retrograde	Gemini
Jun 22	direct	Gemini

Date	Motion	Sign
Jul 11	direct	Cancer
Jul 28	direct	Leo
Aug 12	direct	Virgo
Aug 30	direct	Libra
Sep 26	retrograde	Libra
Oct 18	direct	Libra
Nov 6	direct	Scorpio
Nov 24	direct	Sagittarius
Dec 13	direct	Capricorn

1976

Date	Motion	Sign
Jan 2	direct	Aquarius
Jan 14	retrograde	Aquarius
Jan 25	retrograde	Capricorn
Feb 3	direct	Capricorn
Feb 15	direct	Aquarius
Mar 9	direct	Pisces
Mar 26	direct	Aries
Apr 10	direct	Taurus
Apr 29	direct	Gemini
May 8	retrograde	Gemini
May 19	retrograde	Taurus
Jun 1	direct	Taurus
Jun 13	direct	Gemini
Jul 4	direct	Cancer
Jul 18	direct	Leo
Aug 3	direct	Virgo
Aug 25	direct	Libra
Sep 8	retrograde	Libra

Date	Motion	Sign
Sep 20	retrograde	Virgo
Sep 30	direct	Virgo
Oct 10	direct	Libra
Oct 28	direct	Scorpio
Nov 16	direct	Sagittarius
Dec 6	direct	Capricorn
Dec 27	retrograde	Capricorn

1977

Date	Motion	Sign
Jan 17	direct	Capricorn
Feb 10	direct	Aquarius
Mar 2	direct	Pisces
Mar 18	direct	Aries
Apr 2	direct	Taurus
Apr 19	retrograde	Taurus
May 13	direct	Taurus
Jun 10	direct	Gemini
Jun 26	direct	Cancer
Jul 10	direct	Leo
Jul 28	direct	Virgo
Aug 22	retrograde	Virgo
Sep 14	direct	Virgo
Oct 4	direct	Libra
Oct 21	direct	Scorpio
Nov 9	direct	Sagittarius
Dec 1	direct	Capricorn
Dec 11	retrograde	Capricorn
Dec 20	retrograde	Sagittarius
Dec 31	direct	Sagittarius

Date	Motion	Sign
1978		
Jan 13	direct	Capricorn
Feb 4	direct	Aquarius
Feb 22	direct	Pisces
Mar 10	direct	Aries
Apr 1	retrograde	Aries
Apr 25	direct	Aries
May 16	direct	Taurus
Jun 3	direct	Gemini
Jun 17	direct	Cancer
Jul 2	direct	Leo
Jul 27	direct	Virgo
Aug 4	retrograde	Virgo
Aug 12	retrograde	Leo
Aug 28	direct	Leo
Sep 9	direct	Virgo
Sep 26	direct	Libra
Oct 14	direct	Scorpio
Nov 3	direct	Sagittarius
Nov 25	retrograde	Sagittarius
Dec 15	direct	Sagittarius
1979		
Jan 8	direct	Capricorn
Jan 28	direct	Aquarius
Feb 14	direct	Pisces
Mar 3	direct	Aries
Mar 14	retrograde	Aries

Date	Motion	Sign
Mar 28	retrograde	Pisces
Apr 6	direct	Pisces
Apr 17	direct	Aries
May 10	direct	Taurus
May 26	direct	Gemini
Jun 9	direct	Cancer
Jun 27	direct	Leo
Jul 17	retrograde	Leo
Aug 10	direct	Leo
Sep 2	direct	Virgo
Sep 18	direct	Libra
Oct 6	direct	Scorpio
Oct 30	direct	Sagittarius
Nov 9	retrograde	Sagittarius
Nov 17	retrograde	Scorpio
Nov 29	direct	Scorpio
Dec 12	direct	Sagittarius

1980

Date	Motion	Sign
Jan 2	direct	Capricorn
Jan 20	direct	Aquarius
Feb 7	direct	Pisces
Feb 25	retrograde	Pisces
Mar 19	direct	Pisces
Apr 14	direct	Aries
May 2	direct	Taurus
May 16	direct	Gemini
May 31	direct	Cancer
Jun 28	retrograde	Cancer

Date	Motion	Sign
Jul 22	direct	Cancer
Aug 8	direct	Leo
Aug 24	direct	Virgo
Sep 9	direct	Libra
Sep 29	direct	Scorpio
Oct 22	retrograde	Scorpio
Nov 12	direct	Scorpio
Dec 5	direct	Sagittarius
Dec 24	direct	Capricorn

1981

Jan 12	direct	Aquarius
Jan 31	direct	Pisces
Feb 8	retrograde	Pisces
Feb 15	retrograde	Aquarius
Mar 2	direct	Aquarius
Mar 17	direct	Pisces
Apr 8	direct	Aries
Apr 23	direct	Taurus
May 8	direct	Gemini
May 28	direct	Cancer
Jun 9	retrograde	Cancer
Jun 22	retrograde	Gemini
Jul 3	direct	Gemini
Jul 12	direct	Cancer
Aug 1	direct	Leo
Aug 16	direct	Virgo
Sep 2	direct	Libra
Sep 27	direct	Scorpio

Date	Motion	Sign
Oct 6	retrograde	Scorpio
Oct 13	retrograde	Libra
Oct 27	direct	Libra
Nov 9	direct	Scorpio
Nov 28	direct	Sagittarius
Dec 17	direct	Capricorn

1982

Jan 5	direct	Aquarius
Jan 23	retrograde	Aquarius
Feb 13	direct	Aquarius
Mar 13	direct	Pisces
Mar 31	direct	Aries
Apr 15	direct	Taurus
May 1	direct	Gemini
May 20	retrograde	Gemini
Jun 13	direct	Gemini
Jul 9	direct	Cancer
Jul 24	direct	Leo
Aug 8	direct	Virgo
Aug 27	direct	Libra
Sep 19	retrograde	Libra
Oct 10	direct	Libra
Nov 2	direct	Scorpio
Nov 21	direct	Sagittarius
Dec 10	direct	Capricorn

Date	Motion	Sign
1983		
Jan 1	direct	Aquarius
Jan 6	retrograde	Aquarius
Jan 10	retrograde	Capricorn
Jan 27	direct	Capricorn
Feb 14	direct	Aquarius
Mar 6	direct	Pisces
Mar 23	direct	Aries
Apr 7	direct	Taurus
May 1	retrograde	Taurus
May 25	direct	Taurus
Jun 14	direct	Gemini
Jul 1	direct	Cancer
Jul 15	direct	Leo
Aug 1	direct	Virgo
Aug 30	direct	Libra
Sep 2	retrograde	Libra
Sep 3	retrograde	Virgo
Sep 24	direct	Virgo
Oct 8	direct	Libra
Oct 26	direct	Scorpio
Nov 14	direct	Sagittarius
Dec 4	direct	Capricorn
Dec 21	retrograde	Capricorn
1984		
Jan 10	direct	Capricorn
Feb 8	direct	Aquarius

Date	Motion	Sign
Feb 27	direct	Pisces
Mar 14	direct	Aries
Mar 31	direct	Taurus
Apr 11	retrograde	Taurus
Apr 25	retrograde	Aries
May 5	direct	Aries
May 15	direct	Taurus
Jun 7	direct	Gemini
Jun 22	direct	Cancer
Jul 6	direct	Leo
Jul 26	direct	Virgo
Aug 14	retrograde	Virgo
Sep 6	direct	Virgo
Sep 30	direct	Libra
Oct 17	direct	Scorpio
Nov 6	direct	Sagittarius
Dec 4	direct	Capricorn
Dec 4	retrograde	Capricorn[b]
Dec 7	retrograde	Sagittarius
Dec 24	direct	Sagittarius

1985

Jan 11	direct	Capricorn
Feb 1	direct	Aquarius
Feb 18	direct	Pisces
Mar 6	direct	Aries
Mar 24	retrograde	Aries
Apr 16	direct	Aries

[b]Mercury entered Capricorn on December 4 and went retrograde later that day.

Date	Motion	Sign
May 13	direct	Taurus
May 30	direct	Gemini
Jun 13	direct	Cancer
Jun 29	direct	Leo
Jul 27	retrograde	Leo
Aug 20	direct	Leo
Sep 6	direct	Virgo
Sep 22	direct	Libra
Oct 10	direct	Scorpio
Oct 31	direct	Sagittarius
Nov 18	retrograde	Sagittarius
Dec 4	retrograde	Scorpio
Dec 8	direct	Scorpio
Dec 11	direct	Sagittarius

1986

Date	Motion	Sign
Jan 5	direct	Capricorn
Jan 24	direct	Aquarius
Feb 10	direct	Pisces
Mar 3	direct	Aries
Mar 7	retrograde	Aries
Mar 9	retrograde	Pisces
Mar 30	direct	Pisces
Apr 17	direct	Aries
May 7	direct	Taurus
May 22	direct	Gemini
Jun 5	direct	Cancer
Jun 26	direct	Leo
Jul 9	retrograde	Leo

Date	Motion	Sign
Jul 23	retrograde	Cancer
Aug 2	direct	Cancer
Aug 11	direct	Leo
Aug 29	direct	Virgo
Sep 14	direct	Libra
Oct 3	direct	Scorpio
Nov 2	retrograde	Scorpio
Nov 22	direct	Scorpio
Dec 9	direct	Sagittarius
Dec 29	direct	Capricorn

1987

Date	Motion	Sign
Jan 17	direct	Aquarius
Feb 3	direct	Pisces
Feb 18	retrograde	Pisces
Mar 12	direct	Pisces
Apr 12	direct	Aries
Apr 29	direct	Taurus
May 13	direct	Gemini
May 30	direct	Cancer
Jun 20	retrograde	Cancer
Jul 15	direct	Cancer
Aug 6	direct	Leo
Aug 21	direct	Virgo
Sep 7	direct	Libra
Sep 28	direct	Scorpio
Oct 16	retrograde	Scorpio
Nov 2	retrograde	Libra
Nov 6	direct	Libra

Date	Motion	Sign
Nov 11	direct	Scorpio
Dec 3	direct	Sagittarius
Dec 22	direct	Capricorn

1988

Jan 9	direct	Aquarius
Feb 2	retrograde	Aquarius
Feb 23	direct	Aquarius
Mar 16	direct	Pisces
Apr 4	direct	Aries
Apr 20	direct	Taurus
May 4	direct	Gemini
May 31	retrograde	Gemini
Jun 24	direct	Gemini
Jul 11	direct	Cancer
Jul 28	direct	Leo
Aug 12	direct	Virgo
Aug 30	direct	Libra
Sep 28	retrograde	Libra
Oct 19	direct	Libra
Nov 6	direct	Scorpio
Nov 25	direct	Sagittarius
Dec 14	direct	Capricorn

1989

Jan 2	direct	Aquarius
Jan 15	retrograde	Aquarius
Jan 29	retrograde	Capricorn

Date	Motion	Sign
Feb 5	direct	Capricorn
Feb 14	direct	Aquarius
Mar 10	direct	Pisces
Mar 27	direct	Aries
Apr 11	direct	Taurus
Apr 29	direct	Gemini
May 12	retrograde	Gemini
May 29	retrograde	Taurus
Jun 4	direct	Taurus
Jun 11	direct	Gemini
Jul 5	direct	Cancer
Jul 20	direct	Leo
Aug 4	direct	Virgo
Aug 26	direct	Libra
Sep 11	retrograde	Libra
Sep 26	retrograde	Virgo
Oct 3	direct	Virgo
Oct 10	direct	Libra
Oct 30	direct	Scorpio
Nov 17	direct	Sagittarius
Dec 7	direct	Capricorn
Dec 30	retrograde	Capricorn

1990

Date	Motion	Sign
Jan 19	direct	Capricorn
Feb 11	direct	Aquarius
Mar 3	direct	Pisces
Mar 19	direct	Aries
Apr 4	direct	Taurus

Date	Motion	Sign
Apr 23	retrograde	Taurus
May 16	direct	Taurus
Jun 11	direct	Gemini
Jun 27	direct	Cancer
Jul 11	direct	Leo
Jul 29	direct	Virgo
Aug 25	retrograde	Virgo
Sep 17	direct	Virgo
Oct 5	direct	Libra
Oct 22	direct	Scorpio
Nov 10	direct	Sagittarius
Dec 1	direct	Capricorn
Dec 14	retrograde	Capricorn
Dec 25	retrograde	Sagittarius

1991

Date	Motion	Sign
Jan 3	direct	Sagittarius
Jan 13	direct	Capricorn
Feb 5	direct	Aquarius
Feb 23	direct	Pisces
Mar 11	direct	Aries
Apr 4	retrograde	Aries
Apr 28	direct	Aries
May 16	direct	Taurus
Jun 4	direct	Gemini
Jun 19	direct	Cancer
Jul 4	direct	Leo
Jul 26	direct	Virgo
Aug 7	retrograde	Virgo

Date	Motion	Sign
Aug 19	retrograde	Leo
Aug 31	direct	Leo
Sep 10	direct	Virgo
Sep 27	direct	Libra
Oct 15	direct	Scorpio
Nov 4	direct	Sagittarius
Nov 28	retrograde	Sagittarius
Dec 18	direct	Sagittarius

1992

Jan 9	direct	Capricorn
Jan 29	direct	Aquarius
Feb 16	direct	Pisces
Mar 3	direct	Aries
Mar 16	retrograde	Aries
Apr 4	retrograde	Pisces
Apr 9	direct	Pisces
Apr 13	direct	Aries
May 10	direct	Taurus
May 26	direct	Gemini
Jun 9	direct	Cancer
Jun 27	direct	Leo
Jul 19	retrograde	Leo
Aug 12	direct	Leo
Sep 3	direct	Virgo
Sep 19	direct	Libra
Oct 7	direct	Scorpio
Oct 29	direct	Sagittarius
Nov 11	retrograde	Sagittarius

Date	Motion	Sign
Nov 21	retrograde	Scorpio
Dec 1	direct	Scorpio
Dec 12	direct	Sagittarius

1993

Date	Motion	Sign
Jan 2	direct	Capricorn
Jan 21	direct	Aquarius
Feb 7	direct	Pisces
Feb 27	retrograde	Pisces
Mar 22	direct	Pisces
Apr 15	direct	Aries
May 3	direct	Taurus
May 18	direct	Gemini
Jun 1	direct	Cancer
Jul 1	retrograde	Cancer
Jul 25	direct	Cancer
Aug 9	direct	Leo
Aug 26	direct	Virgo
Sep 11	direct	Libra
Sep 30	direct	Scorpio
Oct 25	retrograde	Scorpio
Nov 14	direct	Scorpio
Dec 6	direct	Sagittarius
Dec 26	direct	Capricorn

1994

Date	Motion	Sign
Jan 13	direct	Aquarius
Feb 1	direct	Pisces

Date	Motion	Sign
Feb 11	retrograde	Pisces
Feb 21	retrograde	Aquarius
Mar 4	direct	Aquarius
Mar 18	direct	Pisces
Apr 9	direct	Aries
Apr 25	direct	Taurus
May 9	direct	Gemini
May 28	direct	Cancer
Jun 12	retrograde	Cancer
Jul 4	retrograde	Gemini
Jul 6	direct	Gemini
Jul 10	direct	Cancer
Aug 2	direct	Leo
Aug 17	direct	Virgo
Sep 3	direct	Libra
Sep 27	direct	Scorpio
Oct 9	retrograde	Scorpio
Oct 18	retrograde	Libra
Oct 29	direct	Libra
Nov 10	direct	Scorpio
Nov 29	direct	Sagittarius
Dec 19	direct	Capricorn

1995

Date	Motion	Sign
Jan 6	direct	Aquarius
Jan 25	retrograde	Aquarius
Feb 15	direct	Aquarius
Mar 14	direct	Pisces
Apr 2	direct	Aries

Date	Motion	Sign
Apr 17	direct	Taurus
May 2	direct	Gemini
May 24	retrograde	Gemini
Jun 17	direct	Gemini
Jul 10	direct	Cancer
Jul 25	direct	Leo
Aug 9	direct	Virgo
Aug 28	direct	Libra
Sep 22	retrograde	Libra
Oct 13	direct	Libra
Nov 4	direct	Scorpio
Nov 22	direct	Sagittarius
Dec 11	direct	Capricorn

1996

Date	Motion	Sign
Jan 1	direct	Aquarius
Jan 9	retrograde	Aquarius
Jan 16	retrograde	Capricorn
Jan 30	direct	Capricorn
Feb 14	direct	Aquarius
Mar 7	direct	Pisces
Mar 24	direct	Aries
Apr 7	direct	Taurus
May 3	retrograde	Taurus
May 27	direct	Taurus
Jun 13	direct	Gemini
Jul 2	direct	Cancer
Jul 16	direct	Leo
Aug 1	direct	Virgo

Date	Motion	Sign
Aug 26	direct	Libra
Sep 3	retrograde	Libra
Sep 11	retrograde	Virgo
Sep 26	direct	Virgo
Oct 8	direct	Libra
Oct 26	direct	Scorpio
Nov 14	direct	Sagittarius
Dec 4	direct	Capricorn
Dec 23	retrograde	Capricorn

1997

Date	Motion	Sign
Jan 12	direct	Capricorn
Feb 8	direct	Aquarius
Feb 27	direct	Pisces
Mar 15	direct	Aries
Apr 1	direct	Taurus
Apr 14	retrograde	Taurus
May 6	retrograde	Aries
May 8	direct	Aries
May 11	direct	Taurus
Jun 8	direct	Gemini
Jun 23	direct	Cancer
Jul 8	direct	Leo
Jul 26	direct	Virgo
Aug 17	retrograde	Virgo
Sep 9	direct	Virgo
Oct 1	direct	Libra
Oct 19	direct	Scorpio
Nov 7	direct	Sagittarius

Date	Motion	Sign
Nov 30	direct	Capricorn
Dec 7	retrograde	Capricorn
Dec 13	retrograde	Sagittarius
Dec 27	direct	Sagittarius

1998

Jan 12	direct	Capricorn
Feb 2	direct	Aquarius
Feb 20	direct	Pisces
Mar 8	direct	Aries
Mar 27	retrograde	Aries
Apr 20	direct	Aries
May 14	direct	Taurus
Jun 1	direct	Gemini
Jun 15	direct	Cancer
Jun 30	direct	Leo
Jul 30	retrograde	Leo
Aug 23	direct	Leo
Sep 7	direct	Virgo
Sep 24	direct	Libra
Oct 11	direct	Scorpio
Nov 1	direct	Sagittarius
Nov 21	retrograde	Sagittarius
Dec 11	direct	Sagittarius

1999

Jan 6	direct	Capricorn
Jan 26	direct	Aquarius

Date	Motion	Sign
Feb 12	direct	Pisces
Mar 3	direct	Aries
Mar 10	retrograde	Aries
Mar 17	retrograde	Pisces
Apr 2	direct	Pisces
Apr 17	direct	Aries
May 8	direct	Taurus
May 23	direct	Gemini
Jun 6	direct	Cancer
Jun 26	direct	Leo
Jul 12	retrograde	Leo
Aug 1	retrograde	Cancer
Aug 5	direct	Cancer
Aug 10	direct	Leo
Aug 31	direct	Virgo
Sep 16	direct	Libra
Oct 4	direct	Scorpio
Oct 30	direct	Sagittarius
Nov 4	retrograde	Sagittarius
Nov 8	retrograde	Scorpio
Nov 24	direct	Scorpio
Dec 10	direct	Sagittarius
Dec 31	direct	Capricorn

2000

Date	Motion	Sign
Jan 18	direct	Aquarius
Feb 5	direct	Pisces
Feb 21	retrograde	Pisces
Mar 14	direct	Pisces

Date	Motion	Sign
Apr 12	direct	Aries
Apr 29	direct	Taurus
May 14	direct	Gemini
May 30	direct	Cancer
Jun 23	retrograde	Cancer
Jul 17	direct	Cancer
Aug 6	direct	Leo
Aug 22	direct	Virgo
Sep 7	direct	Libra
Sep 28	direct	Scorpio
Oct 18	retrograde	Scorpio
Nov 7	direct	Scorpio
Dec 3	direct	Sagittarius
Dec 22	direct	Capricorn

2001

Jan 10	direct	Aquarius
Feb 3	retrograde	Aquarius
Feb 25	direct	Aquarius
Mar 16	direct	Pisces
Apr 6	direct	Aries
Apr 21	direct	Taurus
May 6	direct	Gemini
Jun 3	retrograde	Gemini
Jun 27	direct	Gemini
Jul 12	direct	Cancer
Jul 30	direct	Leo
Aug 13	direct	Virgo
Aug. 31	direct	Libra

Date	Motion	Sign
Oct 1	retrograde	Libra
Oct 22	direct	Libra
Nov 7	direct	Scorpio
Nov 26	direct	Sagittarius
Dec 15	direct	Capricorn

2002

Jan 3	direct	Aquarius
Jan 18	retrograde	Aquarius
Feb 5	retrograde	Capricorn
Feb 8	direct	Capricorn
Feb 13	direct	Aquarius
Mar 11	direct	Pisces
Mar 29	direct	Aries
Apr 13	direct	Taurus
Apr 30	direct	Gemini
May 15	retrograde	Gemini
Jun 8	direct	Gemini
Jul 7	direct	Cancer
Jul 21	direct	Leo
Aug 6	direct	Virgo
Aug 26	direct	Libra
Sep 14	retrograde	Libra
Oct 2	retrograde	Virgo
Oct 6	direct	Virgo
Oct 10	direct	Libra
Oct 31	direct	Scorpio
Nov 19	direct	Sagittarius
Dec 8	direct	Capricorn

Date	Motion	Sign
2003		
Jan 2	retrograde	Capricorn
Jan 22	direct	Capricorn
Feb 12	direct	Aquarius
Mar 4	direct	Pisces
Mar 21	direct	Aries
Apr 5	direct	Taurus
Apr 26	retrograde	Taurus
May 19	direct	Taurus
Jun 12	direct	Gemini
Jun 29	direct	Cancer
Jul 13	direct	Leo
Jul 30	direct	Virgo
Aug 28	retrograde	Virgo
Sep 20	direct	Virgo
Oct 6	direct	Libra
Oct 24	direct	Scorpio
Nov 12	direct	Sagittarius
Dec 2	direct	Capricorn
Dec 17	retrograde	Capricorn
Dec 30	retrograde	Sagittarius
2004		
Jan 6	direct	Sagittarius
Jan 14	direct	Capricorn
Feb 6	direct	Aquarius
Feb 25	direct	Pisces
Mar 12	direct	Aries

Date	Motion	Sign
Apr 1	direct	Taurus
Apr 6	retrograde	Taurus
Apr 12	retrograde	Aries
Apr 30	direct	Aries
May 15	direct	Taurus
Jun 5	direct	Gemini
Jun 19	direct	Cancer
Jul 4	direct	Leo
Jul 25	direct	Virgo
Aug 9	retrograde	Virgo
Aug 24	retrograde	Leo
Sep 2	direct	Leo
Sep 10	direct	Virgo
Sep 28	direct	Libra
Oct 15	direct	Scorpio
Nov 4	direct	Sagittarius
Nov 30	retrograde	Sagittarius
Dec 20	direct	Sagittarius

2005

Date	Motion	Sign
Jan 9	direct	Capricorn
Jan 29	direct	Aquarius
Feb 16	direct	Pisces
Mar 4	direct	Aries
Mar 19	retrograde	Aries
Apr 12	direct	Aries
May 12	direct	Taurus
May 28	direct	Gemini
Jun 11	direct	Cancer

Date	Motion	Sign
Jun 27	direct	Leo
Jul 22	retrograde	Leo
Aug 15	direct	Leo
Sep 4	direct	Virgo
Sep 20	direct	Libra
Oct 8	direct	Scorpio
Oct 30	direct	Sagittarius
Nov 13	retrograde	Sagittarius
Nov 26	retrograde	Scorpio
Dec 3	direct	Scorpio
Dec 12	direct	Sagittarius

2006

Date	Motion	Sign
Jan 3	direct	Capricorn
Jan 22	direct	Aquarius
Feb 8	direct	Pisces
Mar 2	retrograde	Pisces
Mar 25	direct	Pisces
Apr 16	direct	Aries
May 5	direct	Taurus
May 19	direct	Gemini
Jun 3	direct	Cancer
Jun 29	direct	Leo
Jul 4	retrograde	Leo
Jul 9	retrograde	Cancer
Jul 28	direct	Cancer
Aug 10	direct	Leo
Aug 27	direct	Virgo
Sep 12	direct	Libra

Date	Motion	Sign
Oct 1	direct	Scorpio
Oct 28	retrograde	Scorpio
Nov 17	direct	Scorpio
Dec 7	direct	Sagittarius
Dec 27	direct	Capricorn

2007

Date	Motion	Sign
Jan 15	direct	Aquarius
Feb 2	direct	Pisces
Feb 13	retrograde	Pisces
Feb 27	retrograde	Aquarius
Mar 7	direct	Aquarius
Mar 17	direct	Pisces
Apr 10	direct	Aries
Apr 27	direct	Taurus
May 11	direct	Gemini
May 28	direct	Cancer
Jun 15	retrograde	Cancer
Jul 9	direct	Cancer
Aug 4	direct	Leo
Aug 19	direct	Virgo
Sep 5	direct	Libra
Sep 27	direct	Scorpio
Oct 11	retrograde	Scorpio
Oct 23	retrograde	Libra
Nov 1	direct	Libra
Nov 10	direct	Scorpio
Dec 1	direct	Sagittarius
Dec 20	direct	Capricorn

Date	Motion	Sign
2008		
Jan 7	direct	Aquarius
Jan 28	retrograde	Aquarius
Feb 18	direct	Aquarius
Mar 14	direct	Pisces
Apr 2	direct	Aries
Apr 17	direct	Taurus
May 2	direct	Gemini
May 26	retrograde	Gemini
Jun 19	direct	Gemini
Jul 10	direct	Cancer
Jul 26	direct	Leo
Aug 10	direct	Virgo
Aug 28	direct	Libra
Sep 24	retrograde	Libra
Oct 15	direct	Libra
Nov 4	direct	Scorpio
Nov 23	direct	Sagittarius
Dec 12	direct	Capricorn
2009		
Jan 1	direct	Aquarius
Jan 11	retrograde	Aquarius
Jan 20	retrograde	Capricorn
Feb 1	direct	Capricorn
Feb 14	direct	Aquarius
Mar 8	direct	Pisces
Mar 25	direct	Aries

Date	Motion	Sign
Apr 9	direct	Taurus
Apr 30	direct	Gemini
May 6	retrograde	Gemini
May 13	retrograde	Taurus
May 30	direct	Taurus
Jun 13	direct	Gemini
Jul 3	direct	Cancer
Jul 17	direct	Leo
Aug 2	direct	Virgo
Aug 25	direct	Libra
Sep 6	retrograde	Libra
Sep 17	retrograde	Virgo
Sep 29	direct	Virgo
Oct 9	direct	Libra
Oct 28	direct	Scorpio
Nov 15	direct	Sagittarius
Dec 5	direct	Capricorn
Dec 26	retrograde	Capricorn

2010

Date	Motion	Sign
Jan 15	direct	Capricorn
Feb 10	direct	Aquarius
Mar 1	direct	Pisces
Mar 17	direct	Aries
Apr 2	direct	Taurus
Apr 17	retrograde	Taurus
May 11	direct	Taurus
Jun 9	direct	Gemini
Jun 25	direct	Cancer

Date	Motion	Sign
Jul 9	direct	Leo
Jul 27	direct	Virgo
Aug 20	retrograde	Virgo
Sep 12	direct	Virgo
Oct 3	direct	Libra
Oct 20	direct	Scorpio
Nov 8	direct	Sagittarius
Nov 30	direct	Capricorn
Dec 10	retrograde	Capricorn
Dec 30	direct	Sagittarius

Astrological calculations were performed by Janus astrological software (www.astrologyhouse.co.nz) and formatted by Sean Lovatt. This Mercury ephemeris is calculated for Central Standard Time plus six hours—which, including Daylight Saving Time, provides a mean average for those born in the United States. Mercury Retrograde dates may vary by a day in other time zones and parts of the world.

The algorithms used coincide with the Jet Propulsion Laboratories' positions to within 0.1 second of arc and are therefore as accurate as realistically possible. Determining the exact moment a planet goes retrograde is difficult, however, because it is not physically measurable; it must be done mathematically. Slightly different formulas produce time differences of up to fifteen minutes. For instance, one formula might give January 1, 2000, 23.58 and another January 2, 2000, 00.02—a four-minute difference, but a different date.

Mercury Retrograde Periods
2001–2050

Here are the dates for Mercury Retrograde for the next fifty years, plus the Sun sign(s) through which Mercury is traveling. Remember that dates before and after those shown here represent times of Mercury Direct.

This Mercury ephemeris is calculated for Central Standard Time plus six hours—which, including Daylight Saving Time, provides a mean average for those born in the United States. Mercury Retrograde dates may vary by a day in other time zones and parts of the world.

2001

February 3–February 25	Pisces/Aquarius
June 3–June 27	Gemini
October 1–October 22	Libra

2002

January 18–February 8	Aquarius/Capricorn
May 15–June 8	Gemini
September 14–October 6	Libra/Virgo

2003

January 2–January 22	Capricorn
April 26–May 19	Taurus
August 28–September 20	Virgo
December 17–January 6, 2004	Capricorn/Sagittarius

2004

April 6–April 30	Taurus/Aries
August 9–September 2	Virgo/Leo
November 30–December 20	Sagittarius

2005

March 19–April 12	Aries
July 22–August 15	Leo
November 13–December 3	Sagittarius/Scorpio

2006

March 2–March 25	Pisces
July 4–July 28	Leo/Cancer
October 28–November 17	Scorpio

2007

February 13–March 7	Pisces/Aquarius
June 15–July 9	Cancer
October 11–November 1	Scorpio/Libra

2008

January 28–February 18	Aquarius
May 26–June 19	Gemini
September 24–October 15	Libra

2009

January 11–February 11	Aquarius/Capricorn
May 6–May 30	Gemini/Taurus
September 6–September 29	Libra/Virgo
December 26–January 15, 2010	Capricorn

2010

April 17–May 11	Taurus
August 20–September 12	Virgo
December 10–December 30	Capricorn/Sagittarius

2011

March 30–April 23	Aries
August 2–August 26	Virgo/Leo
November 24–December 13	Sagittarius

2012

March 12–April 4	Aries/Pisces
July 14–August 7	Leo
November 6–November 26	Sagittarius/Scorpio

2013

February 23–March 17	Pisces
June 26–July 20	Cancer
October 21–November 10	Scorpio

2014

February 6–February 28	Pisces/Aquarius
June 7–July 1	Cancer/Gemini
October 4–October 25	Scorpio/Libra

2015

January 21–February 11	Aquarius
May 18–June 11	Gemini
September 17–October 9	Libra

2016

January 5–January 25	Aquarius/Capricorn
April 28–May 22	Taurus
August 30–September 21	Virgo
December 19–January 8, 2017	Capricorn/Sagittarius

2017

April 9–May 3	Taurus/Aries
August 12–September 5	Virgo/Leo
December 3–December 22	Sagittarius

2018

March 22–April 15	Aries
July 25–August 18	Leo
November 16–December 6	Sagittarius/Scorpio

2019

March 5–March 28	Pisces
July 7–July 31	Leo/Cancer
October 31–November 20	Scorpio

2020

February 16–March 9	Pisces/Aquarius
June 17–July 12	Cancer
October 13–November 3	Scorpio/Libra

2021

January 30–February 20	Aquarius
May 29–June 22	Gemini
September 26–October 18	Libra

2022

January 14–February 3	Aquarius/Capricorn
May 10–June 3	Gemini/Taurus
September 9–October 2	Libra/Virgo
December 29–January 18, 2023	Capricorn

2023

April 21–May 14	Taurus
August 23–September 15	Virgo
December 13–January 1, 2024	Capricorn/Sagittarius

2024

April 1–April 25	Aries
August 4–August 28	Virgo/Leo
November 25–December 15	Sagittarius

2025

March 15–April 7	Aries/Pisces
July 17–August 11	Leo
November 9–November 29	Sagittarius/Scorpio

2026

February 26–March 20	Pisces
June 29–July 23	Cancer
October 24–November 13	Scorpio

2027
February 9–March 3	Pisces/Aquarius
June 10–July 4	Cancer/Gemini
October 7–October 28	Scorpio/Libra

2028
January 24–February 14	Aquarius
May 21–June 14	Gemini
September 19–October 11	Libra

2029
January 7–January 27	Aquarius/Capricorn
May 1–May 25	Taurus
September 2–September 24	Libra/Virgo
December 21–January 10, 2030	Capricorn

2030
April 12–May 6	Taurus/Aries
August 15–September 8	Virgo
December 5–December 25	Capricorn/Sagittarius

2031
March 25–April 18	Aries
July 29–August 21	Leo
November 19–December 9	Sagittarius

2032
March 7–March 30	Aries/Pisces
July 9–August 3	Leo/Cancer
November 2–November 22	Scorpio

2033
February 18–March 12	Pisces
June 21–July 15	Cancer
October 16–November 6	Scorpio/Libra

2034
February 2–February 23	Aquarius
June 1–June 25	Gemini
September 29–October 21	Libra

2035
January 17–February 6	Aquarius/Capricorn
May 13–June 6	Gemini/Taurus
September 12–October 4	Libra/Virgo
December 31–January 21, 2036	Capricorn

2036
April 23–May 17	Taurus
August 25–September 17	Virgo
December 14–January 3, 2037	Capricorn/Sagittarius

2037
April 4–April 28	Aries
August 7–August 31	Virgo/Leo
November 28–December 18	Sagittarius

2038
March 18–April 10	Aries/Pisces
July 21–August 14	Leo
November 12–December 2	Sagittarius

2039
February 28–March 23	Pisces
July 2–July 26	Cancer
October 26–November 16	Scorpio

2040
February 12–March 5	Pisces/Aquarius
June 12–July 6	Cancer
October 9–October 30	Scorpio/Libra

2041
January 26–February 16	Aquarius
May 24–June 17	Gemini
September 22–October 13	Libra

2042
January 9–January 30	Aquarius/Capricorn
May 5–May 28	Taurus
September 5–September 27	Libra/Virgo
December 24–January 13, 2043	Capricorn

2043
April 16–May 9	Taurus
August 18–September 11	Virgo
December 8–December 28	Capricorn/Sagittarius

2044
March 27–April 20	Aries
July 31–August 23	Leo
November 21–December 11	Sagittarius

2045
March 10–April 2	Aries/Pisces
July 12–August 6	Leo/Cancer
November 5–November 25	Sagittarius/Scorpio

2046
February 21–March 15	Pisces
June 24–July 18	Cancer
October 19–November 9	Scorpio

2047
February 5–February 26	Pisces/Aquarius
June 5–June 29	Cancer/Gemini
October 2–October 23	Scorpio/Libra

2048
January 19–February 9	Aquarius/Capricorn
May 15–June 8	Gemini
September 14–October 6	Libra/Virgo

2049
January 2–January 23	Capricorn
April 26–May 20	Taurus
August 28–September 20	Virgo
December 17–January 6, 2050	Capricorn/Sagittarius

2050
April 7–May 1	Taurus/Aries
August 11–September 3	Virgo/Leo
December 1–December 21	Sagittarius

BIBLIOGRAPHY

Arroyo, Stephen. *Astrology, Psychology and the Four Elements*. Reno, NV: CRCS Publications, 1979.

―――. *Relationships and Life Cycles*. Reno, NV: CRCS Publications, 1979.

―――. *Astrology, Karma and Transformation*. Reno, NV: CRCS Publications, 1993.

Arroyo, Stephen, and Liz Greene. *New Insights in Modern Astrology*. Sebastapol, CA: CRCS Publications, 1991.

Avery, Kevin Quinn. *The Numbers of Life*. New York: Dolphin Books, 1977.

Bailey, Alice A. *Esoteric Astrology*. New York: Lucis Publishing Company, 1971.

―――. *From Intellect to Intuition*. New York: Lucis Publishing Company, 1971.

Bunker, Dusty. *Numerology and Your Future*. West Chester, PA: Whitford Press, 1980.

Campion, N. *An Introduction to the History of Astrology*. London: Institute for the Study of Cycles in World Affairs, 1982.

Carter, C. E. O. *The Zodiac and the Soul*. London: The Theosophical Publishing House, 1960.

―――. *The Astrological Aspects*. Romford, Essex: L. N. Fowler & Co., 1967.

Challoner, H. K. *The Wheel of Rebirth*. Wheaton, IL: The Theosophical Publishing House, 1976.

Collins, Mabel. *Light on the Path*. Wheaton, IL: The Theosophical Publishing House, 1988.

Cunningham, Donna. *The Astrological Guide to Self-Awareness*. Reno, NV: CRCS Publications, 1994.

Edis, Freda. *The God Between: A Study of Astrological Mercury*. New York: Arkana Penguin Books, 1995.

Kelsey, Denys, and Joan Grant. *Many Lifetimes.* New York: Doubleday & Co., 1967.

King, George. *Man's Mind.* Audiotape of lecture. Los Angeles: The Aetherius Society, 1973.

————. *Karma and Reincarnation.* Los Angeles: The Aetherius Society, 1986.

King, George, and Kevin Quinn Avery. *The Age of Aetherius.* Los Angeles: The Aetherius Society, 1975.

King, George, and Richard Lawrence. *Realize Your Inner Potential.* Los Angeles: The Aetherius Society, 1997.

Lawrence, Richard. *Journey into Supermind.* London: Souvenir Press, 1995.

Paramananda, Swami. *Self-Mastery.* Cohasset, MA: Vedanta Center Publisher, 1982.

Peale, Norman Vincent. *The Power of Positive Thinking.* New York: Ballantine Books, 1982.

Ramacharaka, Yogi. *Raja Yoga.* London: L. N. Fowler & Co., 1979.

Schulman, Martin. *Karmic Astrology, Vol. II.* New York: Samuel Weiser, Inc., 1977.

————. *Karmic Relationships.* York Beach, ME: Samuel Weiser, Inc., 1984.

Vivekananda, Swami. *Karma Yoga.* Calcutta: Advaia Ashrama, 1974.

————. *Raja-Yoga.* New York: Ramakrishna-Vivekananda Center, 1980.

Ward, Rutherford. *Pythagoras: Lover of Wisdom.* Northamptonshire, U.K.: The Aquarian Press, 1984.

Wilkinson, R. *A New Look at Mercury Retrograde.* York Beach, ME: Samuel Weiser, Inc., 1997.

Yogananda, Paramahansa. *Where There Is Light.* Los Angeles: Self Realization Fellowship, 1989.

Zolar. *The History of Astrology.* New York: Arco Publishing Company, 1972.

RESOURCES

To obtain a free copy of your birth chart, to learn more about the different types of astrological charts available—personal profiles, relationship charts, forecasts, and so on—or for further information about the study of astrology, please visit www.chrissieblaze.com.

This Web site will also give information about local lectures, workshops, media interviews, and other books by the author.

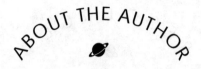

ABOUT THE AUTHOR

CHRISSIE BLAZE qualified as a teacher at the University of London, England. Her professional career has ranged from teaching business studies in London colleges to working as the director of a leading London investment company. She also certified as an astrologer at the Faculty of Astrological Studies, London, and practiced in this capacity in Europe and the United States. Since 1995 she has lived in Los Angeles with her husband, Gary. Through radio and television broadcasts, lectures, and workshops on subjects from astrology to spiritual development to UFOs, Chrissie became a well-known figure in the New Age movement. Chrissie appeared regularly at the Festival for Mind-Body-Spirit, London, and has also appeared at the Whole Life Expo, Los Angeles.

In 1982 Chrissie was ordained in London by The Aetherius Church as one of its first female ministers in England. In 1985 she became public relations officer for The Aetherius Society in Europe and helped launch several successful nationwide campaigns to help raise awareness there. In 1994 Chrissie moved to the American headquarters of The Aetherius Society in Los Angeles to be closer to her Master, Dr. George King, until he passed away in 1997. Chrissie continues as public relations officer for The Aetherius Society in the United States. This allows her to fulfill her goal of the global promotion of practical spirituality.